REJOICE
AND SEE
WHAT HAPPENS NEXT

THE LIFE *and* TIMES *of* TB JOSHUA

KEDMON NYASHA HUNGWE

ISBN 979-8-9860500-0-3 (paperback)
ISBN 979-8-9860500-1-0 (eBook)

CONTENTS

TB JOSHUA MINISTRIES
tbjministries   officialemmanueltv   tbjoshua

AUTHOR'S PROLOGUE

Prophet T.B. Joshua's earthly journey ended on June 5, 2021. It was a beautiful, sunny day when he gracefully entered the stage one more time to bid his people farewell. None in the audience realized that he was speaking his last words on Earth when he said, "Time for everything. Time to come here for prayer and time to return home after service. Watch and pray."

With a brisk walk, he abruptly left the arena. That would be his last walk on Earth.

This book was mostly completed in 2020 and is presented as such. It unfolded as a work of faith with a dawning recognition that T.B. Joshua's ministry was the most consequential event since the days of Christ's apostles. Therefore, this work is a personal testimony of watching and reflecting on the treasure trove of his teachings. He was a teacher par excellence. Through his deep relationship with the Lord Jesus Christ, people witnessed a seamless and powerful connection between the spoken word, signs and wonders, and the quality of life lived.

This book is best read as an outsider's perspective that relies on the wealth of publicly available materials.

My wife and I had the privilege of meeting with Prophet T.B. Joshua on the afternoon of November 26, 2019, having shared a draft copy of the book with him. He graciously embraced our efforts and offered the most generous encouragement, including a financial gift to meet the costs of publication. For that we are forever thankful.

Those interested in reading more about the life and work of T.B. Joshua should also consider Gary and Fiona Tonge's book, *TB Joshua, Servant of God.* They were part of T.B. Joshua's inner circle.

The purpose of T.B. Joshua's life is encapsulated in a message entitled, "The Beauty of Our Achievement."[1] The message is also a pointer for what he passionately believed for others who encountered him. The following are his words.

> It takes faith to maintain your position to the end. The beauty of our achievement is when you are no longer living and the achievement is still there, lingering on in the eyes of and ears of children yet unborn. We are not necessarily blessed by God because of today. It's not necessarily because of today you are blessed, but you are blessed because of tomorrow when you are no longer living. That achievement continues to live so that our children can be influenced in a positive way by our achievement. You will no longer live to educate them, to tell them the right way to follow, but your achievements will be there to talk to them.

> Your concentration is so much on what you want to achieve, what you need. That is your concentration. You want to be this; you want to be that. Vanity upon vanity! If you are known today and you are not known tomorrow, what is the value of it? If your name is written today, and vanishes tomorrow, what is the value? Please think about tomorrow.

PREFACE

This book is based on my encounter with the work of T.B. Joshua of Ikotun-Egbe, Lagos, Nigeria. He had been the general overseer of the Synagogue Church of All Nations (SCOAN).

I have watched thousands of hours of online videos and numerous live services since 2012. I have closely followed press reports and other publications on the ministry. In 2013, following an attendance at an international conference in Abuja, I took some time to make a visit to the SCOAN. This was followed by a second visit in 2015. My wife and I also attended a T.B. Joshua crusade in the Dominican Republic in 2017.

I have been particularly struck by the freshness, vitality, authenticity, simplicity, and power of the SCOAN message. It is my hope that this book will increase our understanding of who God is, the grace of our Lord and Savior Jesus Christ, and the enduring work of the Holy Spirit.

The work of T.B. Joshua encapsulates that great proclamation of our Lord when he declared, "The Spirit of the Lord is on me because he has anointed me to proclaim good news to the poor. He has sent me to proclaim freedom for the prisoners and recovery of sight for the blind, to set the oppressed free." (Luke 4:18 [New International Version])

T.B. Joshua has shown every indication of following this anointed path. He is worthy of careful study and emulation, as our Lord and Master directs, "Verily, verily, I say unto you, He that believeth on me, the works that I do shall he do also; and greater works than these shall he do; because I go unto my Father." (John 14:12 [NIV])

T.B. Joshua has been made out to be controversial and has become the subject of persecution, especially by fellow religious leaders. This is puzzling to me. I have been in his presence and I can say that he is a disarmingly humble, gentle, and generous man.

Some of what is said is out of ignorance, often developing from hearsay and social chatter.

This work is for those that genuinely want to learn. It is my hope that those who are blessed by it will contribute toward the SCOAN charity, Emmanuel TV.

The title of the book, *Rejoice And See What Will Happen Next*, comes from Prophet T.B. Joshua's words during the service of October 13, 2019.

I wish to extend my most sincere gratitude to my wife, Chipo Hungwe, who has encouraged this project. I have gained important insights from our many conversations on the life and work of T.B. Joshua. Her diligent collection of messages and recordings from the ministry has become a treasure trove. She also transcribed most of the video recordings on which the work is based.

Kedmon Nyasha Hungwe
Houghton, Michigan, USA, 2020

THE MYSTERY THAT IS T.B. JOSHUA

A MOST MEMORABLE CRUSADE

On Friday and Saturday, May 8 and 9, 2015, Mexico City witnessed a massive two-day evangelistic crusade that attracted an estimated two hundred thousand people.

The attraction was T.B. Joshua, the general overseer of the Synagogue Church of All Nations (SCOAN) in Lagos, Nigeria. T.B. Joshua has described himself as a prophet and is known as such by those who follow his ministry. The

1. Mexico crusade 2015

Mexico City event provided ample evidence to justify this claim. It was broadcast worldwide on the SCOAN television channel, Emmanuel TV.

By the time the two-day event was over, viewers had witnessed miracle after miracle unfolding before their eyes as T.B. Joshua worked in a seemingly effortless manner through the crowd. Watching him, one was impressed by his matter-of-factly manner and how he seemed to take the unfolding drama as a natural outflow of a Christian life.

He took no credit for what was happening and was at pains to say that he was a mere servant. One would have expected T.B. Joshua to stay on the world stage after this very successful mega event. There was a clear demand for his ministry and his popularity was soaring, certainly in South America.

He had previously held crusades in Colombia and Korea in 2014.

Surprisingly, he disappeared from the public view, leaving the ministry in the hands of his youthful evangelists. They became the face of the ministry on the internationally watched Emmanuel TV. In a statement on the SCOAN Facebook page he wrote, "I came back from the revival trip last week Saturday and am waiting for God's command on what to do next."

He was out of public sight from May until December 2015. These events highlight the enigma that is T.B. Joshua.

I first heard of T.B. Joshua in 2011, but only in passing. When Emmanuel TV went online, I took time to watch the programs. What I saw was a superb teacher whom God was using to reintroduce the power of the Gospel to this generation. He taught with authority and power, using compelling demonstrations that affirmed the full promises of the scriptures.

Over the years I had been taught to believe that the Apostolic Age had come and gone. Yet, I felt there was a contradiction between this understanding and the teaching of our Lord Jesus Christ. While he was on earth, the Lord had said this,

> And these signs will accompany those who believe, in my name they
> will cast out demons; they will speak in new tongues; they will pick
> up serpents with their hands; and if they drink any deadly poison,
> it will not hurt them; they will lay their hands on the sick, and they
> will recover. (Mark 16:18 [NIV])

In 2013, I had occasion to travel to Abuja to attend a professional conference. At the end of the trip, I took the opportunity to visit the SCOAN. I ended up being one of the hundreds of people that met T.B. Joshua in his office. I was surprised that he would be up all night to personally meet with and pray for people. My turn to meet him came up around 4:00 am.

My second visit was with my wife in June 2015, which coincided with T.B. Joshua's birthday. This was the time when T.B. Joshua had gone underground. We were not expecting him to be there and had decided to go there to rest and take time in prayer.

Many newspaper stories had been circulating about his disappearance from the public. We soon realized that he was in the building when he sent a message that we were to be his guests.

We now know that such gestures of kindness were an integral part of his ministry. Indeed, during our stay we met a widow and her children who were also his guests and were staying free of charge. The woman told us that T.B. Joshua's ministry had been caring for her after she lost her husband.

Over the years, we have noted numerous cases of T.B. Joshua's generosity to widows, orphans, the poor, the dispossessed, and refugees. The number of people he cared for was staggering.

He financially supported the building of schools in poor communities in Ecuador and Pakistan; he supported an orphanage in the Ukraine, and he had done charity work in the USA.

He had a huge scholarship program. The better-known beneficiaries are Dr. Yinka Oduwole, whom he sponsored through Oxford University, and Mary-Jean Nleya, a Harvard Law School graduate. They are the tip of the iceberg.

His most enduring work will be in the sustained commitment he had put in place training young evangelists, drawn from across the world. He had the gift of attracting the best and brightest to his ministry.

One may ask where his resources come from. The secret appears to be his giving. He put it this way, "The value of money is not only to build mansions or buy fleets of cars…. The value of money is to use it to help others."

The ministry is supported by a global network of partners who believe in its mission. Some have described him as rich, but my view is that he was well-resourced for his ministry.

T.B. JOSHUA'S HUMBLE ORIGINS

Temitope Balogun Joshua was the last-born child of Kolawole Balogun and his wife Adesiji Kolawole Balogun. He was born in the small village of Arigidi in

Akoko, Ondo State, Nigeria on June 12, 1963. Kolawole Balogun was a farmer and the secretary to St. Stephen's Church in their village.

The pregnancy was difficult and unusual. After nine months his mother went into labor. She was taken to the best hospital, which was in Egbe, Kogi State, for a caesarian operation. However, no surgery was carried out.

One day a pastor came to the hospital and declared, "God is busy preparing this child. So, please, they should not operate you. Go back home. If you attempt the operation, the opposite will happen."

Adesiji called the doctor to whom the message was repeated. The child was eventually born after a fifteen-month-long pregnancy.

As is the custom, a naming ceremony was convened. The excitement was palpable and many came to see this unusual child. The ceremony was violently interrupted. It so happened that there was a group drilling a borehole in a nearby rocky area. A piece of rock flew into the air piercing the roof of the house and landing where the child had lain moments before.

T.B. Joshua had kept the rock. "The stone was supposed to fall on me, but a mysterious force moved me to safety within the same room," he had said.

His mother passed out in shock and was carried to the hospital where she stayed for two days.

He was given some thirty names. He eventually chose to be called Temitope, a Yoruba name that expresses gratitude in view of circumstances surrounding his birth.

His father died when T.B. Joshua was a small boy. Of him, he has said,

> He was an educated man. He lived with the white people as well as serving as church secretary. I cannot say much about my father because he died when I was a small boy. I know that he loved me a lot. I was his pet. I was the one who suffered most from the effect of his death. Being the last born, anywhere he is going, he would take me along. He would carry me to the church. As a little boy, I would be running inside the church. I would jump from the choir to the catechist's table.

After his father's death, his mother was not able to pay for his education. Henceforth, it would be a life of struggle, an experience that has shaped him to be the man he is today. Regardless of the challenges, there were always signs that this was a special child.

A PROMISED CHILD: THE EARLY SIGNS

From 1971 to 1977, T.B. Joshua attended St. Stephen's Anglican Primary School in Arigidi, Akoko. From childhood, T.B. Joshua was passionate about the Bible. Bible knowledge became his favorite subject, and he excelled in it.

He read through the New Testament twice during primary school, and he read the whole Bible during his secondary school, going through it every two months. He became the leader of the Scripture Union. He was known as "small pastor" because of his love for the Bible.

From an early age, he learned to trust in God. This was most dramatically demonstrated one morning when a mad person came to the school, wielding a cutlass. The teachers fled, and the students scattered, but T.B. Joshua, though quite small, stood his ground.

"The Spirit of God spoke to my heart, not to my ear. I heard the voice of God telling me, 'Go there and collect the cutlass. Just tell the madman to bring the cutlass.'"

He moved towards the man and commanded him, "Give me this cutlass, in the name of Jesus."

To everyone's relief and astonishment, the madman surrendered the cutlass to the boy, diffusing a potentially deadly situation.

He would be called on to do prayers at the school assembly, and he would pray for the schools' soccer team.

He had the ability to foretell the results of soccer matches.

Individuals would also come to him for prayer. "It was, pray for me, pray for me, pray for me all the way. They asked me how I was able to overcome the madman and I told them I was surprised myself to see what happened," recounted T.B. Joshua.

Mrs. Margaret Tolani Adejumo was T.B. Joshua's early primary teacher at St Stephen Primary. She could see that he would become a great man.

For his secondary education he was admitted to Ansar-Ud-deen Grammar School in Ikare-Akoko, Ondo State. It was a Muslim school. Christian students were not permitted to carry or read the Bible openly. T.B. Joshua, who was the leader of the Christian group, felt particularly vulnerable. He left within the first year.

> It was obvious I couldn't fit into this dominantly Muslim setting. So, I left the school. I left because my life was in danger. I could sense that since I was doing this thing secretly, one day something could

happen to me. To avoid that I had to leave. From Ikare, I came to Lagos.[1]

He left without informing his mother, travelling with a cassava and cocoa caravan. After four days, he landed in Lagos.

STRIVING AGAINST ADVERSITY

T.B. Joshua arrived in Lagos during the rainy season. His first job was washing the feet of people coming out of the muddy market. One day, he was washing feet when he heard two women conversing in his native dialect. This led to reunification with his sister. He lived with her briefly, but not wanting to be a burden to her, he moved in with a friend and got a new job at a poultry farm.

He was there for a year. His job was to gather and carry chicken droppings. He did not have fond memories of that experience. Within three days, his body odor had changed. "Flies would be hovering around me because I was smelling very badly. There was no amount of bath soap that would remove this odor from my body."

He retained his interest in education, but his circumstances made it difficult to make progress. He would work during the day and attend evening school. He struggled to pay tuition and moved from school to school. In one year, he had gone to six different schools.

In search of something better for himself, he successfully sat for the entrance examination to join the Nigerian Defense Academy. He was invited for a follow-up interview and took a train from Lagos to Kaduna for the appointment. He did not make it.

> Behold, on our journey the train developed some serious faults that kept us in the bush in Jebba for six horrible days with little or no provision…. There was nothing I could do to help the situation as I lacked the means to arrange for an alternative way of transporting myself to the venue of the interview, so I missed the whole thing…. Who knows what would have happened if I had successfully attended that interview. I actually felt very bitter I had missed another chance of making it in life.[2]

He visited his mother and poured out his heart about the many challenges he was facing and the lack of progress in his life. His mother's counsel reassured him and gave him a fresh perspective. She encouraged him to not be distracted by the seeming appearance of his situation.

> Do not be afraid of what the future holds for you, because I know if anyone is destined to fail, you are not the one. So, be patient and you will see what God will do in your life. I am so sure of your future breakthrough, considering the strength of the predictions and prophecies about you even before you were born.[3]

In the face of his challenges, he learned to maintain trust in the God he had believed in from childhood. This became evident to those who came to know him in Lagos.

He rented a very small room on Abati Street. The landlady recognized that he was poor and wondered if he could pay the minimal rental, but he proved to be a memorable tenant.

He loved the little children and would take time to play with them. He established a reputation as a peace maker.

Mr. Abati, after whom the street is named, is one of the people that has fond memories of T.B. Joshua. He used to visit him for prayer and counseling. "People called him Tope then, but when I met him, I called him Prophet…. Because he is so humble, God has lifted him up. I thank God for his life," Mr. Abati has said.

THE CALL FROM GOD

In January 2013, T.B. Joshua published an account of how God called him to the ministry. He did it through a video documentary entitled *This is My Story*.[4] The documentary was introduced during a church service.

> A lot has been said by people concerning how the church Synagogue came into being. Some people questioned my foundation, my mentor, my educational background, and my calling as a man of God. I am not showing this documentary because people questioned my foundation. I am showing this because it is God's time. That is, it is an act of God.

The revelation to start the ministry came during a fast. He prayed and fasted for forty days and forty nights. Concerning this experience, T.B. Joshua says,

I was in a trance for three consecutive days, then I saw a hand that pointed a Bible to my heart. And the Bible entered my heart. And all my heart was immersed with the Bible immediately.

Then the awareness came and I saw the apostles and prophets of old, and someone who I could not see his head because he was tall to the heaven and suspended, which I believe was our Lord Jesus Christ. Seated in their midst, I also saw myself seated in their midst.

After a while, I saw the hand of the same tall man. I could not behold His face which was glittering with unimaginable light. But all the apostles, I could see their faces, particularly apostles Peter and Paul, prophets Moses and Elijah and others. Their names were boldly written on their chests.

I heard a voice saying, "I am your God. I am giving you a divine commission to go and carry out the work of your Heavenly Father."

At the same time, the same hand of the tall Man gave me a small cross and a big Bible, bigger than the one that entered my heart, with a promise that as I keep pressing, in His time and Name, I will be given a bigger cross. But if I fail, the opposite would occur.

I also heard a voice of the same tall man, I could not see his head, saying "I am the Lord your God, who was, and who is, Jesus Christ, giving orders to all the apostles and prophets."

The same voice said to me, "I will show you the wonderful ways I will reveal myself through you, preaching, teaching, miracles, signs and wonders for the salvation of souls."

Since then, I have been receiving in my vision, every year, according to my faithfulness to God, a bigger cross. That means to me, more responsibilities. The Bible that entered my heart symbolizes Spirit and Life.

The first site of his church was at Ogodo, Igbe, Lagos Nigeria, in 1989. Surrounded by a very small outdoor gathering of people, T.B. Joshua announced the founding of the Synagogue, Church of All Nations.

"I don't know where to start," he said. "My coming into your midst is just to lay a foundation. Today we start the Synagogue here."

The announcement was in accordance with the vision God had given him. There was nothing to show that this would lead to the rise of the most watched and celebrated Christian ministry of our times.

A second church was built to accommodate the increasing number of members. The second place of worship was entirely destroyed by a violent thunderstorm. Another building followed. Heavy rain once again caused flooding and destruction. In 1994, the church moved to Ikotun, Igbe, which is the current site.

An archival video shows the construction of the current church building which commenced in 2002. Thousands of people from all over the world, including T.B. Joshua, labored to build the place of worship.[5]

'I AM SENT TO PREACH RIGHTEOUSNESS, WHICH IS CHRISTIANITY'

"I am sent to preach righteousness," were the words of T.B. Joshua in 2000 when he was interviewed by a team from the Netherlands.[6]

He affirmed that the Church was the body of Christ. Jesus Christ was thus the founder of Synagogue, Church of All Nations. "I am just being used. I am a human being just like anyone of us."

When asked if he had received specific directions and plans regarding the future of the Synagogue Church, he replied,

> The future is for Him. He is our future…. He himself is the very future we are talking about. So, concerning the future, the church Synagogue is the church of all nations.
>
> Since He is the answer, there is no limit of what He can do. And there is no limit to His grace. We cannot get beyond God's love. We cannot get beyond God's miracle…. So, you should expect something beyond human understanding.
>
> That is for the future. It is not something that I can stand here and start telling you. There is no amount of words I can use to describe it. So let me say, beyond human understanding.

CHAPTER 2

SELECTED THEMES FROM T.B. JOSHUA

My goal in this chapter is to share what I believe to be the essentials or core principles of Prophet T.B. Joshua's message. This should be understood as a personal interpretation, based on carefully listening to his messages and observing the ministry.

My primary sources have been Emmanuel TV and recordings available on the internet. The record is very extensive and I have struggled with the task of distilling core ideas that I could discuss within the limits of a chapter.

I eventually settled on four themes. The first is from a broadcast entitled *Christianity is a Relationship.*[1] It was delivered to a church audience in January 2013.

The second complementary message has the title *The Secret Behind Miracle*[2] originally published by Emmanuel TV on June 18, 2015.

The third theme is from two messages delivered in 2018 on the subject of the Holy Spirit.[3]

The final and fourth theme is a recurrent teaching on forgiveness.

Prophet T.B. Joshua is not a preacher. Rather, he is a teacher and a superb one at that. There is an edifying power, clarity, and simplicity in all that he says. His tone is conversational. He teaches as one entrusted with an important message. His message re-introduces Jesus to this generation, calling for righteousness in Christ. He frames and presents core ideas from different angles, using illustrations and reinforcement.

Core themes are often reinforced through song. He has the gift of musical composition as well as playwriting. He also has a keen sense of humor. All these qualities are an integral part of his teaching.

His audiences delight in him, but he is uncomfortable when he becomes the point of focus. His point of reference is consistently Jesus Christ. It is also true that his appearance during a service is never guaranteed, for he walks in step with the Holy Spirit. This makes what he has to say of great interest.

I now turn to the messages. The original recordings have been referenced if the reader wishes to follow-up. I do in fact encourage that, if one wishes to get a better experience of the power of the messages.

CHRISTIANITY IS A RELATIONSHIP

In the following message, Prophet T.B. Joshua singularly focuses on Christianity as a relationship. Becoming a Christian is all about entering into a relationship with Jesus Christ. The following are his words.[4]

> I will take you to the book of John 21:15. "So when they had eaten breakfast, Jesus said to Simon Peter, Simon son of Jonah, do you love me more than these? He said yes, you know that I love you. He said, feed my lambs."

> Relationship exists where there is love. Christianity is not a religion. The question you need to ask yourself is, "Are we Christian or religious people going by what is happening?" It is possible for many to put on a mask, or a different face entirely.

> Jesus came to restore the relationship and fellowship between God and man. Take note of this: Where there is relationship, there is fellowship, and where there is fellowship, there is relationship. Where there is relationship there is love.

> Nothing will keep us on course better than a deep love for the Lord. Nothing will carry us through the hardship like a sincere devotion to Christ.

> Ministry does not begin with a relationship with people. It begins with a relationship with God. That relationship overflows to people.

When you have a relationship with people, you must know where that relationship flows from. First to God then to human beings.

In the book of John 21:15, it is very surprising that the Lord Jesus did not ask Peter, "Do you love people?" Loving people is important for ministry, loving God is more important.

Are you with me? Jesus did not ask Peter if he was a gifted speaker or a talented leader. He did not ask Peter about seminary training or the Bible college he attended. Those things are important but they are not the issue. To give eloquent speech, to be a gifted speaker or leader are important but they are not the issue. Being able to quote the Bible from Genesis to Revelation is very important but that is not the issue.

The issue is quite simple. The basic qualification for lasting ministry is found in Jesus's question "Do you love me?" In other words, do you have a relationship with me? That is the question Jesus is asking you.

The church today has been taken over by man's natural gifts. Speaking skill, and the ability to inspire have taken over the church. That brings Satan to beat the drum in the church of God.

Man exhibits natural gifts, talent and education, when you can speak very well and you can speak the Word of God. This has reduced God's kingdom to human knowledge.

Using man's natural gifts to do God's work is dangerous and challenging in the church today. There is nothing bad with talent, but man's natural gifts--education, ability, talent-- must be obedient to God's will before you can receive God's blessing.

Take your time to study the book of 1 Corinthians 12:7-8.

"But the manifestation of the Spirit is given to each one for the profit of all. To one there is given through the Spirit the message of wisdom, to another the message of knowledge by means of the same Spirit, to another faith by the same Spirit, to another gifts of healing by that one Spirit, to another miraculous powers, to another prophecy, to another distinguishing between spirits."

The supernatural gifts of the Spirit given to a believer are separated from man's natural gifts, and man's natural abilities such as talent and education. Let me give a good example. If I want to talk by man natural gift, it is my human nature that will do it. I will teach but my human nature will take it over which is different from when I am under the control of the Holy Spirit.

Take your Bible to John 14 vs. 26. "But the helper, the Holy Spirit whom the Father will send in my name will teach you all things and will bring to your remembrance all things that I say to you."

Here the Holy Spirit teaches as He wills. The Holy Spirit teaches, prays, fasts, witnesses, and testifies as He wills. But man has the ability to teach, man has the ability to pray, man has the ability to testify. He is doing this without corresponding power. He is doing this without the support of Heaven. He loves doing it. When you love something, you must also receive the corresponding agreement.

Man has the ability to testify, to go out and preach, to go out and witness without the corresponding power. One would not be under the control of the Holy Spirit. He can say "I am here to pray the Word of God to you." But he is the one testifying. Jesus never sent him. He is doing this without the support of Heaven. He loves doing it.

When you love something, you must also receive the corresponding agreement to say, "Okay this is for you." So, the challenge the church is facing now is that the ministry of God cannot be reduced to human knowledge. That is, man's natural gifts, talent, ability, education. Those things are important but they are not the issue. The issue is quite simple. The basic qualification for lasting ministry is found in Jesus's question "Do you love me? Do you have a relationship with me?"

The main thing about Christianity is not the work we do but the relationship we maintain and the atmosphere produced by that relationship. Yes, you have a passion for God but it's not enough to go to theology school to study the Bible. You can study the Bible but what of the relationship? You have to build this relationship.

What we do for God is only a reflection of the relationship we have with God. If we want to be able to do great things, we need to have a great relationship.

If you want to have a ministry that is strong, your relationship must be strong with God. Going by that test from John 21, ministry does not begin with a love for people but begins with a love for God and that love overflows to people. This message tells you that you should straighten your life.

Never you forget that ministry does not begin with the love for people. If you say you love me you must love God first. And if you don't love God and you say you love me, where does the love flow from? If you say you have a relationship with me as a pastor, you must first have the relationship with God.

Nothing will keep you on course like a deep love for the Lord. You should be ready for good times and hard times. It is only your love for Christ that can keep you going when there is no money in your pocket. If not, you begin to see Jesus in a bad light.

When everything seems to be confused, and it seems to be trouble everywhere, it is your love for Christ that will keep you going. What can separate me from the love of Christ? Can someone answer me? Can sickness separate me? No. Affliction? Depression? Hardship? No, No. What can separate you from the love of Christ?

THE SECRET BEHIND MIRACLES

In this section, Prophet T.B. Joshua's primary focus is on the phenomenon of prophecy, healings and deliverance. He explains how and why these are a natural outflow of a ministry that is in step with the Holy Spirit. The section is based on two messages: "The Secret Behind Miracle"[5] delivered at the Synagogue Church of All Nations, and a message delivered at a pastors conference in Colombia in 2014.[6]

There are five core ideas that constitute the message: 1) belief in Jesus Christ is a matter of the heart, and it is through such belief that we are saved; 2) the Word builds Christ nature into those who believe; 3) believing is possessing; 4) why are miracles not happening in the church today; and 5) what is the way forward? The words of Prophet T.B. Joshua follow.

It Is with the Heart That We Believe

With the heart, man believes that Jesus is his righteousness. God's righteousness which is a gift from above boasts in the finished work of our Lord Jesus Christ while self-righteousness boasts in itself. "If you declare with your mouth, 'Jesus is Lord,' and believe in your heart that God raised him from the dead, you will be saved. For it is with your heart that you believe and are justified, and it is with your mouth that you profess your faith and are saved." (Rom. 10:9-10 [NIV])

"If you believe in your heart that Jesus is Lord, you are saved. He who believes has eternal life." (1 John 5:13 [NIV]) We are saved by a gospel that tells us that Jesus Christ died on the cross for our sins and rose from the dead. Hearing this Word and embracing it by faith is what saves us.

The blood that He shed on the cross of Calvary is the most precious commodity in the history of humankind. The blood He dripped from His hands, His feet and His head.

The Word Builds Christ Nature into Us

The Word dominating you is the Lordship of Christ in you. When you are calling the name Jesus, it is the Word dominating you which is equivalent to Christ personally being in you. The Word dominating you is the Christ you are calling. (1 Cor. 2:4; 1 Thess. 1:5 [NIV])

If there is no indwelling Word, and you are calling the name Jesus, you are calling Him in vain. Jesus will not come to the scene if His Word does not dominate or rule you.

The Word builds Christ nature into individuals. (Acts 20:32 [NIV]) In other words, God is building Himself into us, making Himself a part of us, as the Word dominates, rules and sanctifies our spirit nature. The power that flows from His name will be in proportion to your love for His Word.

When that love is expressed, don't be surprised to see things change, things loosed, and things bound. Don't be surprised to see signs and wonders. The Spirit is released to the degree we stand in reverence of His Word.

Believing Is Possessing

Believing is possessing. The instant you believe, you have. How can you believe? You can believe in your heart when you not only hear the Word with your ears, but also in your heart. To hear God's Word with our heart requires openness and hunger for God's Word. See God's Word as if your life depends on knowing it.

Indeed, our lives depend on knowing it. If the Spirit is not joined to yours, your words are today's language. We use today's language to gossip, to talk to our children, to do business, sing songs, give orders and directives.

The truth that cannot heal, cannot save, can we regard as truth? It is faithless, a photocopy truth.

Why Are We Not Seeing More of God's Power in Today's Church?

People ask me why miracles, healing, prophecy are not happening everywhere. God is going to withhold the phenomenon of signs and wonders until two things join or coalesce. What are the two things? The Word and the Spirit. You can be sound in doctrine and be lost. You can know the Word and be lost and not be converted.

The power that flows from the name Jesus will be in proportion to our love for His Word. The Word dominating you is what you are calling when you say, "In the name of Jesus." It is the Word dwelling in you which is equivalent to Christ personally being in you.

The power that flows from His name will be in proportion to our love for His Word. There is power in our mouth. When you preach, Jesus comes onto the scene. And when Jesus comes onto the scene, He performs miracles. When Jesus comes onto the scene, signs and wonders follow. If you have not realized your power, it means the proportion of your love cannot release the power.

When you say, "In the name of Jesus" and nothing is released, that means the Word in you is dormant. It is the love of Christ that heals and love of Christ that blesses. If one does not love, one cannot be entrusted with this grace.

Jesus is saying we cannot continue to talk, speak, preach about the two, the Word and the Spirit in separation. When we look at what is happening in the ministry today, churches are known for one or the other. It is either this church is known for the preaching, teaching; the other is known for miracles, signs and wonders. This is not how it should be.

Jesus was "a prophet, powerful in Word and deed, before God and all the people." (Luke 24:vs 19 [NIV]) That is our standard. The early church stood strong in the doctrine and the power of the Lord. The same thing should happen today.

In the next paragraph, T.B. Joshua reiterates the point that Christianity is a relationship. The collective failure on this essential principle accounts for the lack of power in the church today.

The union of the Word and the Spirit has been challenged by modern day circumstances. What are the challenges? Man's natural gifts. Ability, talent, and education. People study the Word today and believe it is all. But the main thing about Christianity is not the work we do, but the relationship we maintain and the atmosphere that brings about the Spirit.

Today, we preach the Word alone without being carried along by the Spirit. That is why the name Jesus we call seems to be inactive, seems to be idle, seems to be meaningless, because we are not being carried along. We pray without the Spirit of God. We preach without the Spirit of God. We teach without the Spirit of God. People will hear you, we will entertain people, but God will not hear us. When we preach without being carried by the Spirit, we preach of ourselves; we entertain people. This is the challenge we are having today.

Our Future as Christians

Our future as Christians depends on learning from each other. What you have, and I do not have, give me. What I have, and you do not have, I will give you. What I have, and you do not have, makes you to envy me, and fight me and call me all sorts of names. What I have and you have makes me to envy you and fight you. Our reward as ministers of God is peace of heart. Peace of heart is contentment. Seek first the kingdom of God, not the crowd. What is the kingdom of God? The Spirit of God.

"[T]hey will pick up snakes with their hands; and when they drink deadly poison, it will not hurt them at all; they will place their hands on sick people, and they will get well." (Mark 16:18 [NIV]) What does that mean to you? This means nothing until we act on the Word. How do we act on the Word? By meditating and turning over and over what we have read in our heart. The more you think about what you have read, the more you become familiar with His voice.

Nothing will happen until we act on the Word. But today we go by what we read. It says, "They shall lay their hands on the sick and they shall recover."

So, people are now laying their hands on the sick without the Spirit of God. "They shall lay their hands on the sick and they shall recover" means nothing until we act on the Word.

Looking into and acting on the Word brings Jesus on the scene. When you say, "in the name of Jesus," and you are not looking, and acting on the Word, Jesus will not come to the scene. People you pray for will hear you. You will hear yourself. Jesus will not hear you.

Believe and Be Filled With the Holy Spirit

In 2018, Prophet T.B. Joshua delivered two messages on the subject of the Holy Spirit. The first one was "Knowing Jesus, Knowing the Holy Spirit"[7] and was followed by "Believe and Be Filled With the Holy Spirit."[8]

Citing John 16, in the first of the two messages, he said it was, "perfectly plain that the Holy Spirit is the One that reveals Jesus to us."

Consequently, Jesus cannot be known without knowing the Holy Spirit. He declared that Jesus was Spirit, and His worshipers must do so in spirit and truth. The following words are also from the same message.

Man's spirit is dead because of sin. The natural man, that is the man of mind and intellect, cannot understand nor receive things of the Spirit. There has been a great mix-up in the Church. It is the erroneous assumption that spiritual truths can be intellectually perceived.

It is possible to grow up in the church and learn all rites but not know Jesus.

In John 16, it is perfectly plain that the Holy Spirit is the One that reveals Jesus to us. You can read your New Testament and still never find Jesus in it. You can be convinced that Jesus is the Son of God and still never find Jesus. You can be a publisher of the Bible; you can know about Christ dying for you; you can head this or that religious organization, and still never know Jesus of Nazareth in the power of the Holy Ghost.

In the Church, there are two Christs, the Christ of story and history and song—the baby Jesus. Then there is the Christ whom the Holy Spirit reveals. Many people know about Christ, but they don't know Christ. There is a difference between knowing about Christ and knowing Christ. In John 3:27, "No man can receive except it is given from above."

If you are reasoned into Christianity and claim to be a Christian without the Holy Ghost, some wise fellow can reason you out of it unless you know the Holy Spirit. Christianity stands or falls on the illumination of the Holy Ghost. It is either the Holy Ghost or darkness. The Holy Ghost is God's imperative of life. If our faith is to be a New Testament faith, if Jesus Christ is to be the Christ of God, rather than the Christ of history or story, the illumination of the Holy Ghost will tell our hearts that we are learning at Jesus's feet, not at man's feet.

In the follow-up message, "Believe and Be Filled with the Holy Spirit," Prophet T.B. Joshua followed up on this theme. He opened by re-stating the problem in these words.

How can we believe in order to be filled with the Spirit of God? That is the question you need to ask yourself. It is difficult to live right without being filled. You cannot obey the written Word without being filled. Without being filled, it's like you are without a helper because the Holy Spirit is our helper. How can one live without a helper in times of temptation? No one can do the work of obedience, but God does as He wills. You can do it as a man, but for reasons known only to you.

Drawing on the teachings of Jesus Christ from the Gospel of John, Prophet T.B. Joshua emphasized the role of the Holy Spirit as the believer's Helper.

> In John 7:37-39, Jesus said, "If you believe in Me, you will receive the Holy Spirit." The question you need to ask yourself is: did you receive the Holy Spirit when you believed?
>
> Jesus said those who believe in Him would receive. It is His will for every believer to be filled with the Holy Spirit. Without the Holy Spirit, you cannot live right. You cannot obey Him. You cannot obey the Bible. It's not possible. Wherever Jesus is glorified, the Holy Spirit comes. Without being filled, you cannot glorify Him. Wherever Jesus is honored, the Holy Spirit comes. You cannot honor Him without the Holy Spirit. How will you honor Jesus without the Holy Spirit?
>
> There is truth in God's Word. Without being filled with the Holy Ghost, you cannot understand that truth. There is healing, deliverance, blessing, and salvation in God's Word. But all these can be unveiled to you when you are filled with the Holy Ghost. A Christian not filled with Holy Ghost is a Christian without a Helper. In times of tribulation, no Helper. In times of temptation, no Helper. In times of trial, no Helper. To stay with Jesus is to stay with the Holy Ghost. In times of temptation, tribulation crisis, that is where our safety lies. When you call Jesus without being filled, you cannot see Jesus on the scene.

Prophet T.B. Joshua then turned to the heart of the matter as he talked about the work of faith. By this he means a faith based on acting on the Word. The crisis in the church arises from double lives, as people live contrary to what they profess. Such lives "quench" the Spirit. This is a matter that Prophet T.B. Joshua has taught with utmost passion and concern, describing the state of the church as "very, very painful."[9] The following text clarifies his thinking.

Believe and Be Filled

> The Bible says in John 7:37-39, "If you believe in Me, you will receive the Holy Ghost."
>
> But if I start there, it will be difficult for you to understand what

I am talking about. But the whole thing comes from faith. If you believe in God in a certain matter, you should have a work of faith in that matter. Faith is expressed through work and by this work faith is perfected. But many of us today don't know how to believe and express our faith. Faith without work is dead. And what is that work?

Let me give you a good example. After prayer you believe it is not going to rain, and at the same time you carry an umbrella along. What is the umbrella you carry for, as a Christian? This nullifies your faith. This is a form of unbelief. Inconsistency of your belief makes you to carry an umbrella in case it rains. This means our heart is uneasy and restless. This shows that we have not yet believed. When one believes, he is at rest. When a person believes, he will no longer worry or doubt. You pray over some trouble, but you are busy planning on your own solution. You are worried and full of anxiety as if you have never prayed at all. You run to a specialist, or to a professor who is specialized in a certain matter. After leaving the place, you now run to quack people, those who kill people, to treat you again. Tell me why this quack thing will not spoil the work of the specialist.

God is not a man. Only faith pleases Him. A prayer of faith must be followed by an absolute trust in God that He is now working out the answer.

In the message, "Knowing Jesus, Knowing the Holy Spirit"[10] Prophet T.B. Joshua had warned of the dangers of a wavering faith.

Jesus is in the power of the Holy Ghost. If you have learned to worship one Man, you will not worship other men. Because you don't know Jesus, that is why you can run to spiritualists. You keep running, because you have not learned to worship one Man.

If you are not filled with the Spirit of God, you cannot obey the written Word. And if you cannot obey the Bible, you quench Him. If your faith is to be a New Testament faith, if Jesus is to be the Christ of God, rather than the Christ of history and stories, then the illumination of the Holy Spirit will tell your heart that you are worshipping Him and you are learning at His feet.

How Then Should We Pray?

Your prayer is one-sided. You never hear from Him. It's only you who always talks. Prayer is two-sided conversation. You talk, and Jesus talks. Do you hear from Him? Your heart is not a dwelling place yet. You have to prepare your heart. There is a conflict between the flesh and the Spirit. There is a division. Get your heart set by meditation. Hymns, spiritual songs, melodies. Get your heart ready. He will soon enter and when He enters you will just see prayer coming naturally. Not the one you form by yourself.

Many of us claim to be believers without being filled. You are a Christian without a Helper because you are not yet filled. It's a crisis. If you are not yet filled, you can be a Christian as you proclaim, without a Helper. He helps us in our struggles. You need a Helper in times of temptation, and tribulation, because He promised He will not leave us without the Helper

FORGIVENESS

Prophet T.B. Joshua has taught that the heart is the contact point for the Holy Spirit. It must be free to function as an instrument of the Holy Spirit. Among the factors that he has fixed attention on is offence. Offence may be understood as an unforgiving spirit, pain of the past, hatred, and bad feelings towards others. Prophet T.B. Joshua made offence the centerpiece of his 2016 New Year prayer. These were his words.[11]

Offence is the effective instrument used by Satan to trap us, to imprison us, to make us bond servants. Just because you were mistreated, just because you were wrongly accused, or lied against, you do not have permission or right to hold onto offence. As we all know, offence is a trap of the enemy. We are usually shocked, surprised and bewildered when offended as if we are the only one wronged. Jesus made it abundantly clear that it is impossible to live among people, to live this life, and not have the opportunity to be offended. I mean, it is impossible that no offence should come. It is not a question of opportunity to be offended, but what your response will be. Your response determines your future.

The theme of forgiveness has been an established and recurrent theme of T.B. Joshua's ministry. One of the earlier messages on forgiveness was delivered on February 23, 2012.[12] It is instructive to share the extended text. The following are T.B. Joshua's words.

We shall dwell on forgiveness. What is forgiveness? You have many meanings of forgiveness. When you read your Bible, forgiveness means that God looks at you as if you had never sinned. When you receive His forgiveness, you are blameless before Him. God's forgiveness does not sweep your sin under the carpet. Instead, He completely washes them away. Your friend may say I forgive you and tomorrow say, 'No, no, no.' His forgiveness completely washes your sin away.

Let's look at the Book of Matthew 5:44. "But I say to you, love your enemies, bless those who curse you, do good to those who spitefully use you." Forgiveness paves the way for a harmonious relationship even with your enemy.

How can you forgive someone who has hurt you deeply? Let's go to the book of Matthew 6:14. "For if you forgive men their trespasses, your Heavenly Father will also forgive you. But if you do not forgive men their trespasses, neither will your Father in heaven forgive your trespasses."

If you forgive someone who sins against you, your Heavenly Father will forgive you. If you refuse to forgive others, your Father in Heaven will not forgive your sin. How does this strike your mind? Being unwilling to forgive shows that you have not understood or benefitted from God's forgiveness. If you have been forgiven, that forgiveness will create in you a forgiving heart towards others. Going back to Matthew 5 verse 44, it says love your enemy and bless those who curse you.

That is, love your enemy and pray for those who persecute you. How does this appear to you? When you love your enemy and pray for those who hate you, this releases you from the destructive emotions of anger, bitterness, revenge and others. Can you see the importance of loving your enemies and praying for those who persecute you?

In Luke 23:34 Jesus said, "Father forgive them, for they do not know what they are doing."

Jesus forgave even those who mocked and killed Him. We should be more concerned about our offenders and their relationship with God and less about nursing our own grudges, self-pity, or ill will. The person most hurt by unforgiveness is you.

As a Christian when you have something against a fellow brother, you are not settled, you are disturbed in your heart. You cannot go to God for any prayer. An unforgiving attitude not only destroys your relationship, but also poisons your soul. The person most hurt by unforgiveness is you not your enemy.

As a Christian, there is no way you can pray. Even if you pray you only hear yourself. God will not hear you. "Don't repay evil with evil." (1 Pet. 3:9 [NIV])

Don't retaliate with hurt. Instead, when people hurt you, pay them back with blessing. That is what God has called us to do and He will bless us for it.

Ephesians 4:31 says, "Let all bitterness, wrath, anger, clamor and evil speaking be put away from you with all malice."

What does this mean? It means that when people say hurtful things about you, God wants you to respond by blessing them. Look at the case of our Lord Jesus Christ. Jesus forgave those who mocked and killed him. What is the lesson for you and I?

We should be more concerned about our offenders and their relationship with God, and less about nursing our own grudges, self-pity and ill will. If you fail to receive forgiveness and forgive those who sin against you, you also will find yourself in a torture chamber. You will find yourself having to be everything, do everything and accomplish everything totally in your own strength, ability and intelligence. And since that is never possible, you will be under high stress and emotional torture.

You will work hard and struggle greatly but never achieve any progress. If you become great and you have something against your fellow brother, it means that greatness will be used against your fellow brother. Being unwilling to forgive shows that you have not understood or benefitted from God's forgiveness. It is only by the mercy and compassion of God.

Who needs forgiveness? First forgive yourself before you can forgive those who sin against you. Begin to forgive yourself and forgive those who sin against you.

CHAPTER 3

FORGIVENESS IS THE KEY

This chapter presents case studies from the SCOAN where the principle of forgiveness has been taught and applied to change lives and situations and to restore broken relationships. As T.B. Joshua has taught, letting go of offence allows the Holy Spirit to work in people's lives and in their situations.

CASE 1: MRS. MEMORY CHIRINGAKUDENGA FINDS A NEW CAREER AFTER BEING SACKED[1]

Mrs. Memory Chiringakudenga from the United Kingdom was sacked from her job as a result of a false accusation. She was devastated and embittered. The experience was particularly harrowing because she was the breadwinner for her family. She knew the people who had made the false allegations against her. Although she turned to Emmanuel TV for support, she could not find a way out of her desperation and depression.

She decided to write T.B. Joshua, pouring out her pain. On the Sunday following that communication, the Prophet gave a message entitled "The Benefit of Failure."[2] He said he had been reading emails, and Memory Chiringakudenga immediately recognized that the message was for her.

In her testimony, she recalled the Prophet teaching that, difficult situations we find ourselves in are meant to take us to the next level, regardless of what those situations may be. After hearing the message, Memory Chiringakudenga decided to visit the SCOAN for prayer. However, the message she received there was unexpected and difficult. God expected her to forgive those who had hurt her. She was in turmoil over the message, but in the end, she decided to submit and leave things to God.

With her heart free, the voice of God spoke clearly to her. She was to stop working for others and stand on her own feet. She did not know how this would work but God had a plan. She was led to a business partner with whom she established a care company. Within weeks the company was established.

The people that instigated her sacking from her previous job sought to derail her initiative. They were not able to prevail. When it became clear that her venture was succeeding, some of her enemies sought to join her as employees.

She refused to hold onto offence and hired them. She had come to realize that forgiveness is not a choice but a command of God. When she testified at the SCOAN she owned a large company with over thirty branches across the United Kingdom.

CASE 2: MRS. SUZANA MJUWNI DISCOVERS THE RICH BLESSINGS OF FORGIVENESS[3]

Mrs. Mjuwni from Malawi was a troubled woman when she first visited the SCOAN. A superior at her workplace had made serious but false criminal allegations against her. The issue was tied up in the courts, and her career had come to a standstill. She was desperate. She had also faced threats to her health, but this did not appear to be uppermost in her mind when Prophet T.B. Joshua unexpectedly approached her during the church service.

T.B. JOSHUA: How are you madam? Pray against operation.

MRS. MJUWNI: Okay.

T.B. JOSHUA: There is an object that is moving in your stomach.

MRS. MJUWNI: Yes, man of God.

T.B. JOSHUA: There is time you went for tests because your menstruation had ceased.

Mrs. Mjuwni confirmed that. She also said that someone had given her anointed water from the SCOAN and the menstruation resumed. By now she could tell that the Prophet had deep knowledge of who she was. But he had still not touched upon what was uppermost on her mind. Prophet T.B. Joshua then turned to the issue of her job, but not in a way that she had anticipated.

T.B. JOSHUA: Can you forgive this man?

Although the identity of the man was not mentioned, it's likely that she immediately knew what he was talking about. The direction of the conversation was awkward and unexpected. She was the aggrieved party.

MRS. MJUWNI: Yes, I will forgive him.

T.B. JOSHUA: Wait, wait. I am going into your life. I am just taking it step by step. Can you forgive this man?

MRS. MJUWNI: Yes.

T.B. JOSHUA: Because twice he took you to court.

The precision of the exchange was breathtaking. She broke down in tears.

MRS. MJUWNI: [crying uncontrollably] Yes, up until now the case is not yet over. I still need to go to court man of God. It has actually stopped my career. It ceased. I have even brought the files here.

T.B. JOSHUA: But you are not the one that explained to me. I am just telling you what I am seeing.

MRS. MJUWNI: You are a true man of God. You are my father in the Lord.

T.B. JOSHUA: [laughing] You are my mother in the Lord. If I am your father in the Lord, you are my mother in the Lord. Ok, it's alright. Don't worry.

T.B. JOSHUA: [he took her hand] You just take the step of forgiveness and see what happens.

MRS. MJUWNI: I have forgiven him.

T.B. Joshua then prayed for her. And then a miracle happened. This was only revealed much later after she had returned home, and then came back to the SCOAN to give a testimony.

This time she was a transformed woman. She looked bright and happy. During her testimony, she gave more details about the court case that was brought up through prophecy. A false allegation of corruption had been made by her senior. The case had been dragging in the courts for four years. After her SCOAN visit, she had called the man and asked for forgiveness.

Immediately after that, her situation changed. She unexpectedly received an offer for a position with the Southern African Development Community (SADC) Secretariat. She had not applied for the position. She was now a diplomat, and the job was much bigger than her old job.

Furthermore, the High Court in her country had reviewed the charges against her and determined that the case should be annulled. This, despite the efforts of her detractor to continue pressing the false charges. This was a clear case of God taking over the situation and acting on her behalf when she obeyed the command to forgive.

CASE 3: MARRIAGE RESTORED[4]

This was a case of an adulterous relationship where a man showed up in church with a married woman who was not his wife. She was in fact his friend's wife. The Spirit of God rescued the situation. Prophet T.B. Joshua dealt with the issue with gentleness and kindness. A transcript of the encounter is provided to show the directness and power of the prophetic encounter.

T.B. JOSHUA: Can I speak to you?

MAN: Yes, sir.

T.B. JOSHUA: You need to reconcile your home. Where is your wife?

MAN: At home, sir.

T.B. JOSHUA: But you are here with one woman.

MAN: Yes, sir.

T.B. JOSHUA: Who is the woman?

MAN: [the other woman is by his side] She is right here, sir.

T.B. JOSHUA: [pointing to the woman] You?

WOMAN: Yes, sir

T.B. JOSHUA: He is here with you?

WOMAN: Yes, sir.

T.B. JOSHUA: But you are somebody's wife.

WOMAN: Yes, sir

T.B. JOSHUA: Your husband is at home.

WOMAN: Yes, sir.

T.B. JOSHUA: [to the man] Give me your hand. What a handsome man. What a beautiful woman.

T.B. JOSHUA: [to the woman] You know at the beginning your husband was not poor like this.

WOMAN: It is true, sir.

T.B. JOSHUA: At the beginning he had money. He was taking care of the home.

WOMAN: Yes, sir.

T.B. JOSHUA: But now, no money.

WOMAN: It's true.

T.B. JOSHUA: And you know you are the one who lured this brother. You brought this brother to this life. This brother was helping you before you started going out with him.

WOMAN: It's true, sir

T.B. JOSHUA: I want to see you. Don't worry. I want to see the husband of the other woman. The marriage is from God. I still want her to go back to that house. The wife of this gentleman I also want to see. I want to see them privately.

This is classic T.B. Joshua. No judgment. Does this not remind one of our Lord, Jesus Christ whom T.B. Joshua has so closely imitated?

The husband of the woman came to the church at a later point. He was inconsolable, weeping bitterly.

> MAN: Man of God, help me. Because I don't have money! Look at what my wife has done to me. The person I love and taken care of. I can't live with this woman again. I am tired of her. I can't believe this is my life. Oh my God!

> T.B. JOSHUA: Many marriages are like this, without revelation.

> MAN: Man of God, please. Can I live with this woman again?

> T.B. JOSHUA: It's like you are blaming God for revealing this. It is never her will. It is the sin in her. Let her be delivered from that sin so that you people will live together again. It's only when you can say that you have never done this in your life that you can say you will never forgive this woman. It is one of those things you have to pass through. Forgive her, because you too need forgiveness. She has realized her mistake. Forgive her and forgive the man.

The woman then approached the husband pleading for forgiveness. He was inconsolable, bitter, and sorrowful.

> MAN: [they were both wailing] Why did you do such a thing? It's not easy for me.

After much persuasion and encouragement, the bitterness and pain yielded. Prophet T.B. Joshua prayed for them.

In a follow-up message T.B. Joshua had more to say on the matter.

> The reason forgiveness is so important is that relationship does not involve two perfect people. You must continue to forgive because you need to be forgiven. There is no such thing as a perfect relationship. Those people don't exist on this earth.

> When we talk forgiveness, this is what our Heavenly Father does on our behalf. It was a debt that could never be paid in a person's lifetime. No matter how many good works we do, we cannot do enough to earn God's forgiveness. It is only through the mercy and compassion that we are forgiven.

The man's name was Livinus Asogwa and she was Ifeoma Asogwa. He was thirty-five years old. They had been married for fifteen years and had five children. When T.B. Joshua learned that they had so many children and that they were so young and poor he rebuked them for being irresponsible.

He nevertheless offered the man a job at the church. The church also provided an apartment and scholarships for the children to go back to school. They also received a cash gift of three hundred thousand naira.

CASE 4: A WAYWARD MAN FINDS HIS WAY BACK[5]

This is the case of Velma Garland and her ex-husband Carl Garland who showed up at the SCOAN, all the way from the United States. They were divorcees, after thirty years of marriage. Velma explained how they had ended up in Nigeria.

> I was looking on television and I came across YouTube. I saw Emmanuel TV. I was watching the testimonies that were very compelling. I live in the United States and this is Africa, and I have never been to Africa.
>
> I was watching deliverance. I was watching demons manifesting, and these people were talking about how God had reconciled them after the deliverance. I felt like if I can get here that maybe God could do the same thing for me and my marriage.

God honored her faith. They were sitting separately in the church auditorium, with Carl in the front row and she sitting behind him. As he moved around praying for people, T.B. Joshua prayed for her. When he saw Carl, he had a revelation about their story.[6]

T.B. JOSHUA: Who is she to you?

CARL GARLAND: That's my ex-wife of thirty years …

T.B. JOSHUA: There is a divorce, and you are the cause.

CARL GARLAND: Yes, I am.

T.B. JOSHUA: At a time, God was blessing you with money, you messed up the whole thing. You go out looking for women.

CARL GARLAND: Yes, I messed up.

T.B. JOSHUA: At a time when things were very difficult, she was with you.

CARL GARLAND: I wasted thirty years.

T.B. JOSHUA: You have not seen anything unless God restores this marriage. I need to see you. This is sickness. [speaking to the ex-wife]

WIFE: Yes, yes.

It later turned out that he had infected her with sickness because of his promiscuity.

T.B. JOSHUA: This is sickness. It is sickness.

He prayed for both of them and was gone to the next person.

The following week the couple spoke to the congregation about their experiences. Velma Garland spoke first. She spoke of how her husband had lost

2. Carl and Velma Garland reconciled

his way and began to womanize. She suffered much humiliation and abuse. "Women were calling me and leaving messages on my phone. One even had the nerve to tell me that she had been seeing him for seven years."

The affairs were numerous. The final straw was when he infected her with disease. She filed for divorce. After T.B. Joshua prayed for them at the SCOAN, she had seen changes in Carl. She saw repentance and humility.

> The arrogance was not there. Affection for me came back. He acted like he cared for me again. Then yesterday, we went to the prayer mountain, and we began praying and I began to speak in my heavenly voices. Next thing I know, he began to speak in tongues. He got filled with the Holy Spirit.

T.B. Joshua listened to their testimony and followed with a teaching. The following is a condensed version of his remarks.

> Satan causes people to lose control. He lost control. But now he has come to his senses. This is why you have to cultivate a habit of forgiveness. When you are under bondage and you are released, you see the true color of yourself.

> That is why the Lord says forgive and forget. You have to learn to forgive. Whatever anyone might have done to you, please forgive and forget. I know it is not easy when you are not delivered. It's spiritual. You must be released. And when you are released, you will see the need for forgiveness.

> Love is from the heart. The love that comes from the heart is the love that can build marriage. When the love comes from the heart, it does not mean that there will be no tribulation. Trouble strengthens our life. Think about what I said. Fire removes impurities from gold. Without fire, you cannot discover what we call gold. In the same vein, problems strengthen your life.

> God's plan for our life causes us to face problems. When problems come, you overcome and are promoted. Without problems you remain on the same spot. We run from the very thing that brings strength to our life.

Your problem could be persecution, could be hatred, sickness, and just name it. If you are looking for a smooth marriage, you need to go to Heaven. That the marriage is settled does not mean the crisis has stopped. Strength comes to marriage through trouble. As disagreement comes, strength comes. That is just life.

CHAPTER 4

THE THREE VISITORS

The Synagogue Church of All Nations attracts thousands of visitors from within Nigeria and from across the continents. They have come from all walks of life. Others have been most impressed by high profile visitors, such as leaders of countries. In this chapter, my focus is on three visitors who came as a result of revelation about T.B. Joshua and his ministry.

Each of these men served to affirm that T.B. Joshua was called by God as a prophet for this generation. They arrived at the SCOAN from Africa, the United States, and New Zealand, at separate points in time. But their message was the same. They are Francois Van Zyl of South Africa, Evangelist C. S. Upthegrove (1928- 2018) of the United States, and Evangelist Bill Subritzky (1925-2015) from New Zealand.

PASTOR FRANCOIS
VAN ZYL OF SOUTH AFRICA

South African Francois Van Zyl was one of the earliest visitors to the church. He spoke of his visit to a SCOAN congregation on May 9, 1999. He arrived at the SCOAN after traveling across the world in search of a deeper meaning and experience of the gospel of our Lord, Jesus Christ.

> I just want to tell you that I gave my life to Jesus about twenty-four years ago. And while I was a young Christian, I took the Bible and I looked in the Bible, and I saw many Scriptures in the Bible that

talked about the power of God. And I saw scripture where Jesus said you will do the things I have done and even greater things you will do. Then when I read the Bible, I said, God, yes, it is true, but I have never seen it in my life.

I have been in the ministry now for twenty-four years. For twenty-four years I have prayed and said, "God, I am looking for the anointing. It must be somewhere." About five years ago, God spoke to me clearly and said go into the world and look and you will find a man of God and you will find what I want to give you from him.

He listed numerous countries he had visited including Lesotho, Malawi, Botswana, Namibia, Zimbabwe, the United Kingdom, Germany, Holland, Belgium, Italy, Spain, Greece, Canada, United States, Brazil, and Argentina.

So, I have travelled, and I believe today from the depth of my heart, and I am honest with you, this is the place that God wants to meet with me. God said to me, "Go and find a man who is anointed. Go and speak to him and let him pray for you. Then go back to your country and also pray for the sick."

I see that Scripture is being fulfilled in the last days like it says in the Bible where Jesus says, "These things you shall do, but also you shall do greater things because I am going to Heaven, to my Father and I am going to send you the Holy Spirit and the Holy Spirit will give you the power to do these things."

I am not surprised that God is using a Black man. If you go and look the way Jesus chose his disciples, he did not say, "let me go to the university and get wise people." He did not go to the synagogue and say show me the people that are praying the most; show me the people that are highly educated; show me the people that went to your Bible schools; I want the best people too for my team.

No. He went to the seaside and got people from the boats. Those were fishermen. He also went and chose a tax collector.

If you travel all over the world, you will find many people that proclaim that they are Christians. The Bible says they have got a form of godliness, but they do not have the power. So therefore, when the power comes, they will be jealous and they will say, "but that cannot be God; it must be Satan."

Because if they say that it is God, then they accuse themselves. According to Scripture, if a kingdom is divided against itself, it will fall. Our warfare is not against flesh and blood but it is against the principalities. The Bible also says that the devil will come as an angel of light and he will try and steal the glory of God. But he will not succeed because he is a liar.

Van Zyl also had a special message for the ministry. He urged Prophet T.B. Joshua and the Synagogue Church of All Nations to be outward looking and to be faithful in sharing the Word to the whole world. He said, "The Bible also says as we give, we shall receive."

Therefore, when God starts to speak to Prophet T.B. Joshua, and God tells him to move out, to go wherever God wants him to go, you people need to let him go. Why? Because God says as you give, He will give back to you even more.

I also want to tell you a Scripture, and you must tell me if it is the truth or not. In the Bible it says in John 3:16 that God the Father so loved the world that he gave His only begotten Son so that the world may be saved.

And you know, when Jesus anointed the disciples, they wanted to stay in one place. They didn't want to go and preach the Gospel to the whole world, but you know what happened? They were persecuted, and they were forced to go into the whole world and preach the Gospel.

This anointing that is here, if you don't allow the Holy Spirit to take Prophet T.B. Joshua when God calls him and tells him to go, persecution will come on this church and God will see that you all go into all the world because there are people out there who have HIV /AIDS, they have cancer, they are dying. They are dying without Jesus. So, what God has given you, you have got to give it away. Why? So that God can multiply it back to you.

If you look at scriptures, where Jesus fed the 5,000, he gave the bread to the disciples. When did the bread multiply? When he prayed? No. When he gave it to the disciples? No. But when the disciples took the bread and started giving to the 5,000 it started to multiply. So, we have got to give. Whatever we have, we have to take it out and we have to give it. We cannot keep it to ourselves.

EVANGELIST BILL SUBRITZKY OF NEW ZEALAND (1926-2015)

Evangelist Bill Subritzky visited the SCOAN from New Zealand. He originally came in the early days of the ministry when T.B. Joshua was becoming known and was beginning to attract criticism from the religious establishment.

Bill Subritzky re-appeared at the SCOAN in March 2014. It was immediately evident that T.B. Joshua had the highest regard and deepest affection for him. He referred to Subritzky as his father in the Lord. He introduced the evangelist with a brief word.[1]

When the going was tough, he stood by me. In the past, he stood by me because of principle. The Book of Romans 3:1-4 says, "Let God

3. Evangelist Subritzky and his wife Kaylene

be true but every man a liar." Indeed, everyone tells lies to his neighbor. Whom can we believe? But we can still believe true servants of God and God Almighty. Here you meet a true servant of God, my father in the Lord.

Evangelist Subritzky came to the podium and spoke more about his relationship with T.B. Joshua. He was accompanied by his wife, Kaylene. He had this to say:

On March 10, 1971, as a practicing lawyer and businessman, a very successful one, I went to an evangelist meeting. I didn't believe in healing but there I saw a person touched mightily by the power of God. I gave my life to Christ in that meeting. I was born again of the Spirit of God, turned 180 degrees from darkness to light, from the power of Satan to the power of God, and God called me into evangelism, even though I was in business and law. For the next thirty years, I traveled to many countries, held thousands of crusades and spoke to thousands of people over those years. After thirty years, I thought I knew it all. When you think you know it all, you are in trouble.

Eleven years ago, somebody gave me a DVD of the meetings in the SCOAN and the tremendous healings. I was astounded. I mean, I had seen healings, cast out demons and written books on it. I was regarded as an authority on it but I had never seen the likes of it.

People were beginning to criticize [T.B. Joshua] in the western world and say that the people who were claiming to be healed were not the same people who were prayed for. All sorts of lies began to develop in the western press about our brother.

So, I felt I should come here. The Holy Spirit said, "Come here. Bring some pastors with you and bring your sons and check it all out because this is a man of God."

We spent ten days here, listened to T.B. Joshua, and saw great meetings, healings and miracles. I took back fifteen DVDs with me and began to reprint and distribute them by the thousands in our country and other countries. The criticism went on but the Holy Spirit kept saying, always, "This is a man of God. Support him."

I thank God for Prophet T.B. Joshua. As he mentioned, the criticism was terrible, but at the same time he has weathered the storm. He has come through. The enemy is defeated and God has won the victory. So, I want to pay tribute today.

When I left the SCOAN after receiving impartation from Prophet T.B. Joshua, I called a public meeting. Immediately after receiving the impartation, I received a power that I had never known in thirty years of ministry. I began to see people miraculously healed.

I am not boasting. The power of the Holy Spirit imparted through our brother Prophet T.B. Joshua radically transformed my ministry. As a result of that and over subsequent crusades, I have seen many thousands of people come to Christ and seen them healed in the name of Jesus. So, my ministry was totally transformed by the power of God through Prophet T.B. Joshua, the man of God. Today I want to honor him.

I have listened to his theology. When we went back, all the pastors that were with me checked his theology and we were very satisfied that he was teaching the truth about Jesus Christ which he was criticized. We praise God for it.

I believe today is a special day. It is an honor for me to be here and to honor Prophet T.B. Joshua in your midst. I am going to suggest now that we all stand for one moment in this place. Can we all stand for a moment?

If you are watching on TV, I am going to ask you to participate. What I am going to do is ask everybody to put their hand out towards the platform, towards Prophet T.B. Joshua. We, as the body of Christ, are going to honor him at this moment.

Father, we come in the name of Jesus Christ, as the body of Christ, and we thank you for the millions who have entered the Kingdom through the ministry that You have given Prophet T.B. Joshua. We thank You, Lord, for the millions who are yet to enter the Kingdom. We pray for dear Prophet T.B. Joshua, his wife Evelyn and their family, for your mighty blessing to be upon them in the days to come, in health, strength and for that wonderful anointing that he has to be imparted to many others. At the same time, we pray that anointing will even increase more in the days to come.

We thank You for this mighty work that You have accomplished through him. Father we thank You that the Kingdom of God is being extended hourly through this mighty ministry. Bless him Father, strengthen him and in every way, anoint him as a special servant of Yours.

We give you all the glory, in the name of Jesus Christ, and everybody says, Amen!

EVANGELIST C. S. UPTHEGROVE
OF THE UNITED STATES (1928- 2018)

The third notable visitor was Evangelist C. S. Upthegrove (1928- 2018).[2] He came with his daughter Brenda. At the time of his visit, he was eighty-three years old and had been preaching the gospel for over sixty-eight years.

T.B. Joshua appeared awed and honored that this elderly man would come all the way to Lagos to meet him. He would not even introduce the visitor to the

4. Evangelist C. S. Upthegrove

congregation when he spoke. T.B. Joshua introduced him by saying, "Looking at our father, you know he is our grandfather. I will not stand here as a boy and begin to introduce grandpa. Let grandpa talk. You are welcome, sir."

It was indeed a captivating story.

"I am Evangelist C. S. Upthegrove from the United States of America. I want to thank God for the privilege of being here in Africa for the first time," the old man said with a characteristic twinkle in his eye and a booming voice that belied his advanced age. "And I am walking on Holy ground!" he declared.

He continued:

Many years ago, when I was working with great men of God like A. A. Allen, William Branham, Oral Roberts, R. W. Shambach, great men of the past, God gave me an opportunity to stand on their shoulders.

And I was riding one day in the automobile with A. A. Allen and he looked over at me and said, "Brother Upthegrove, I may not be living when this comes to pass, but I believe you will."

And he began to describe this place. He began to talk about a man that would walk out under the anointing and the power of the Almighty God.

He further described all the miracles I have witnessed since I have been here. On Thursday, when the Wise Men began to minister, I couldn't help but sit there and weep because of the fulfilment of the prophecy that the man of God had given me.

A. A. Allen said, "Brother Upthegrove, there will be a multitude of people from all over the world that will hear simultaneously," and this was many years before the technology we have now. There was no internet.

He further began to tell me about the anointing and the power that was going to come upon such men as Prophet T.B. Joshua. In the middle of the 60s, in 1966, he began to describe to me the mannerism in which the Spirit of the Lord would fall. When I walked into this place, the Spirit of the living God witnessed to me and said, "You are walking on holy ground."

Brother Allen further said to me, "Brother Upthegrove, when you see this begin to happen, know that the time is near to the making up of the Bride, without spot and without wrinkle."

The man of God told me …[that] I would move in the spiritual realm and see these things come to pass, [and] God would make provision for me to go and see for myself. I thank God for the privilege, and for the way being made for me to be in this place right now. Ever since I have been here, I remembered what I first saw on Emmanuel Television, as this man of God began to move in supernatural realms. I saw the prophecies that came to pass.

Make no mistake about it, you are living in the presence of a mighty prophet sent from God. God said to me, as I was watching this man on Emmanuel television, "This is my prophet."

And he said "I am establishing around the world twelve anointed apostles and prophets. And he said to me, T.B. Joshua will be one of the twelve prophets that God will establish around the entire world. When God told me that, I said, "Oh Lord, make a way for me. I want to be there."

In concluding his message, C. S. Upthegrove read a prepared message that the Spirit of God had given him for T.B. Joshua and especially for those present.

Behold my son, I speak to you in this very hour. A door will be opened to you like never before. Thou hast asked and I have heard thy prayer. I have begun to prepare dignitaries from around the world to accept thy vision.

From this very hour you are appointed as one of the twelve prophets that I will establish around the world to usher in the Bride of Christ without spot or wrinkle. Thou hast truly followed the example of my own Son. When you bless the sick and the poor, you have done it unto me.

I will restore everything that the cankerworm and the palmerworm and the caterpillar, and the locust hath eaten away, even to the bark of the tree.

You will see my hand move not many days hence. You are my end time messenger and appointed prophet for this hour, to usher in the Bride of my Son. Thus, saith the Lord.

During his visit, C. S. Upthegrove appeared to have an intimation that his earthly journey was soon coming to an end…. With him on the piano, together with his daughter, they produced a wonderful rendition of the song, "Goodbye World."

I've told all my troubles goodbye
Goodbye to each tear and each sigh
This world where I roam cannot be my home
I'm bound for that home in the sky
I walk and I talk with my Lord
I feast every day on His word
Heaven is near and I can't stay here
Goodbye world, goodbye

This was indeed the end of one era, and the beginning of a new one. A passing of the baton. C. S. Upthegrove's death was announced on January 28, 2018.

UNDERSTANDING PROPHETIC MINISTRY

That T. B. Joshua can be called a prophet has been a matter of controversy among some people. The following quote from Wikipedia is typical of how this has been discussed.

> SCOAN claims that Joshua has successfully predicted events in the lives of individuals who attend his church services as well as worldwide events, including a purported prophecy of Michael Jackson's death, and the outcome of two African Cup of Nations (AFCON) final matches, which were won by Zambia and Nigeria respectively. He has been voted by the public among the most famous prophets.

T. B. Joshua has sought to educate people on what it means to be a prophet. His explanation goes beyond the narrow popular view that focuses on predictions of events. In a message entitled, "Who is a Prophet,"[1] he said the following.

> The belief of people is that a prophet is only out to predict or foretell the future. That is why people are not used to prophets.

> There are two classes of prophets. There are those who have the ability to communicate the saving will of God to others. These may be called general practitioners, or general prophets. They are true

preachers and true teachers because of their deep knowledge of the Scriptures. They preach and teach about things both announced and known to protect you and to guarantee your life.

The other prophets are those who receive direct and specific messages from God. We have them in the Bible. In 2 Samuel 12, Nathan rebukes David for adultery and murder. David repents. In 1 Kings 18, Elijah has a showdown with the prophets of Baal on Mount Carmel. In 2 Kings 7, Elisha predicts that the siege of Samaria would be lifted, and it came to pass.

The belief of people is that a prophet is only out to predict or foretell the future. The prophet also has the grace to tell you the situation at the moment. Whom you are, whom you were, and whom you shall be.

When you read the Bible, prophets advise and correct kings and queens, political and religious figures. These are the people that receive direct and specific messages from God. They are not general practitioners.

In this chapter I present compelling evidence that demonstrates that T. B. Joshua is a prophet entrusted with the higher level of grace. He receives direct and specific messages from God. These messages inform people of whom they are, whom they were, and whom they shall be. Such prophecies are the bedrock of the work of his work. They have the power to show people the face of Christ and compel them to put their trust in Him. This prophetic gift receives no attention from outside critics. The numbers of persons who have received such prophecies are too numerous to count.

In this chapter, I provide a very limited sample. In the next chapter, I present examples of world prophecies that focus on geopolitical events. World prophecies have attracted the attention of the wider world and especially the press. Nevertheless, they are of marginal significance to T. B. Joshua's core mission of winning souls to Christ.

Prophetic encounters with T. B. Joshua can be quite awkward, confusing, or embarrassing. The persons receiving a word of prophecy are often caught off guard and unprepared for what they hear. In many cases, they will have come to the church looking for blessing for their plans or something along those lines.

Questions such as "where is your wife?" or "where is this child?" have often brought up shocking and complicated details from a buried past. Some of that was evident in Chapter 3 which focused on offence and forgiveness. The prophetic word goes to the root of their problems and swiftly brings resolution to troubled lives and situations. The first case I will present is of a young American woman. After her encounter with Prophet T. B. Joshua, she introduced herself as Elysia Straub.[2]

CASE 1: ELYSIA STRAUB IS RESTORED[3]

Elysia Straub had a bedwetting problem since childhood. She was now an adult woman. Her sense of shame was overwhelming. She hid the problem from the staff at the SCOAN when asked what she wanted to be prayed for. She hoped the problem would quietly go away during prayer. But that was not God's plan for her. She was sitting in the church auditorium when T. B. Joshua suddenly turned to her. She seemed willing to talk until she saw the direction he was taking.

T. B. JOSHUA: Can I talk to you?

ELYSIA STRAUB: Yes.

T. B. JOSHUA: There is an embarrassment in your life.

T. B. JOSHUA: [Elysia looks stunned] Do you know what I mean by an embarrassment?

T. B. JOSHUA: [silence. Elysia looks very uncomfortable] It is not something you can tell anyone.

T. B. JOSHUA: [silence] Something you don't want anyone to know.

T. B. JOSHUA: [silence] It's only you. You keep it to yourself and you don't want people to know.

ELYSIA STRAUB: Yes, sir.

T. B. JOSHUA: You want me to mention it?

T. B. JOSHUA: [Elysia shook her head] You don't want me to mention it?

T. B. JOSHUA: [silence] No, let's put shame to Satan.

T. B. JOSHUA: Bedwetting.

ELYSIA STRAUB: [tearfully] Yes, sir.

T. B. JOSHUA: As I am saying it, it's gone.

Prophet T. B. Joshua prayed for her. She came back the following week with a testimony of victory. Gone was the reticence to talk.

5. Elysia Straub testifies at the SCOAN

"People of God, I have good news to share," she said. "I have had this problem since childhood." She was accompanied by her mother. The problem was indeed gone, and she was full of joy.

My next case is of a bishop who found himself receiving a message about a very secret life. Once again, I use transcripts as the best way of presenting the prophetic interactions.

CASE 2: A BISHOP IS RESTORED

During a live service, T. B. Joshua suddenly turned to a man sitting in the audience with a request to speak to him. There was no evidence in his appearance or attire that he was a man of the clergy. As usual, T. B. Joshua's interactions were direct and pointed, going to the root of the matter. His directness can be shockingly personal for those not acquainted with him. But it is a directness borne out of deep love for people and comes with no judgment whatsoever.

T. B. JOSHUA: Where is your wife?

MAN: [inaudible response]

T. B. JOSHUA: Because you have challenges.

MAN: Yes.

A SECOND MAN: Man of God, he told me about this.

MAN: Yes. I have challenges. All my life. No child.

T. B. JOSHUA: No, don't worry. Don't bother to get sympathy. Because I know what I am talking about. Because they want you to go from one woman to another. This is the third woman.

MAN: [exclaiming in shock] Oh! The Lord has spoken!

T. B. JOSHUA: [laughing] OK. Don't worry.

He moved on, but was not done with him, and he came back.

T. B. JOSHUA: You shouldn't be shy. You go out with a woman, and since then your penis has gone. You cannot meet your wife again. You cannot tell your wife what happened. You keep going to hospitals, buying drugs. You knew that the day you met this woman. A fat woman. After you finished with the woman, your penis shrunk. You don't even have feeling when urinating, talk less of erection.

He touched him to impart healing and he was restored. The church invited his wife, and they appeared together the following week. They testified of the of the challenges they had faced, and the restoration received.

CASE 3: AN ADULTEROUS MAN BRINGS THE OTHER WOMAN TO CHURCH[4]

In another event, a word of prophecy exposed a married man who had come to church with a girlfriend. The man in question was not even inside the church auditorium but was outside the building in the overflow section.

T. B. JOSHUA: There is a brother under the canopy. Your wife is at home, and you are here with a lady. What kind of prayer do you want to offer? What do you hear us preaching since morning? Your wife is at home. She is even trying to cook food for you, but you are here with one lady. For salvation or for what? If you don't come out, you are here to tempt me. If you tempt a man of God, you know the repercussions. You have to come out. Salvation first. You will not be able to help yourself. God loves you. Thank you.

After a while the man comes into the building and walks to the front of the auditorium.

MAN: Man of God, I am the man that came here with my girlfriend while my wife is at home.

T. B. JOSHUA: What has your wife done to you?

MAN: She didn't do anything.

T. B. JOSHUA: And she is beautiful. You like her?

MAN: Yes.

T. B. JOSHUA: It is this urge.

T. B. Joshua then said he wanted to have a private meeting with the man and his friend after the service. A week later, the man returned, this time with his wife. He asked his wife to forgive him in front of the live audience.

MAN: I am sorry, baby.

THE WOMAN: My name is Chioma Kelechukwu. On Tuesday I got a call that man of God and Emmanuel TV want to see me. I came and they explained what is happening. I was surprised and did not know what to do. I trusted my husband and did not know he could do such a thing. Nevertheless, to God be the glory. I thank God and Emmanuel TV for helping me recover my home.

CASE 4: A WOMAN BETRAYED

The next case is a sad story of a Nigerian man who travelled to Gabon, met with a local French speaking woman and struck a relationship. When she became pregnant, he abandoned her and the child and left for the Democratic Republic of Congo. There he met another woman whom he married. He had four children with her.

He had come to the SCOAN for prayers because he faced business-related challenges. However, the prophetic word took him back to his messy past, forcing him to confront the pain he had caused. He ended up meeting the daughter he had rejected. The man's name was Elijah Chikwendu. The transcript of the encounter follows.

> T. B. JOSHUA: How are you brother?
>
> ELIJAH CHIKWENDU: [inaudible, he moved nearer T. B. Joshua]
>
> T. B. JOSHUA: Are you the one that betrayed this woman, or she betrayed you?
>
> ELIJAH CHIKWENDU: I am the one.
>
> T. B. JOSHUA: [shaking the man's hand] Thank you. I am happy. This is a Christian. How did you betray her?
>
> The man explained that he had travelled to Gabon and had a relationship with a woman who became pregnant and had a baby girl.
>
> T. B. JOSHUA: You know at the beginning of that baby girl; you were trying to deny it.
>
> ELIJAH CHIKWENDU: Exactly.
>
> T. B. JOSHUA: Even your voice is still not clear concerning that child.
>
> ELIJAH CHIKWENDU: Yes.
>
> T. B. JOSHUA: The child is living with her mother.
>
> ELIJAH CHIKWENDU: Yes, sir.

The church sought out the daughter and brought her to Lagos. She was accompanied by her mother. The church covered the cost of international travel and provided lodging and meals. Twelve years had passed, and the child was meeting her father she had never known for the first time. T. B. Joshua was delighted. He has regularly expressed a sense of wonder at the ways God has used him.

"I am just a servant," he has said.

> T. B. JOSHUA: Can you see the power of prophecy? This beautiful girl would have been lost. It was that prophecy that made him to agree that he is the father.

> ELIJAH CHIKWENDU: Man of God, I need your help.

> T. B. JOSHUA: These are the things blocking many of you. You are seeing her for the first time. But you are looking for breakthrough. For blessing. Ninety-nine percent of challenges are caused by ourselves. Many of you don't know the cause of your problems. That is why, no matter the prayer you offer, your prayer cannot be answered. Because something is there that needs to be removed. If you fast for forty days, forty nights, go to the prayer mountain, nothing will happen. Many of you want to say I am a Christian now. I started to be faithful and kind. You were a drunkard and you stopped drinking. You were a liar, you stopped lying. You were a thief, you stopped stealing. You started living a good life and people say you are Christian now. But your life has not changed. There is a hindrance. But people say, 'this man has stopped going to nightclubs. He is now going to church. He is even an elder in the church. He fasts, he is an usher, he is everything. He is preaching. But life has not changed.' Why? All that kindness, goodness, God is not hearing it. Until that hindrance is removed.

Speaking to Chikwendu, T. B. Joshua counseled him to take up his responsibilities as a father and make sure his daughter was in school. He was to repay the mother for the cost she had incurred educating the child. He then talked to the daughter through translation, because she spoke French. He asked her why she had not wanted to get close to the father when she met him at the church.

> LITTLE GIRL: [tearful] Because he abandoned me.

> T. B. JOSHUA: Oh! Don't let her talk again. Please.

He gave here some encouraging words and said he would meet with her after the service.

CASE 5: PROSTITUTE RESTORED[5]

Erefe Bubemi from Delta State, Nigeria found herself at the SCOAN during a Sunday service. She came all the way from Cameron where she had gone to live as a prostitute. However, she became tired of the life. Attempts to drown her pain with alcohol and partying had not worked.

An acquaintance directed her to the SCOAN for help. The person paid for her travel to Lagos. God had mercy on her, and the Spirit of God directed T. B. Joshua to call her out from among the thousands who attended the Sunday church service. This is how the interaction unfolded.

> T. B. JOSHUA: There is a woman there. You are a prostitute. You have a wig on your head of different colors. Please come out. If you can be among the children of God, I think it is time to quit and give your life to God. She is there! Jesus loves you.

Erefe Bubemi came forward, wearing a huge colorful wig of brown and white colors.

> EREFE BUBEMI: I am the prostitute woman you called out. I am a prostitute. I smoke. I drink. I go to clubs. I meet with men.

> T. B. JOSHUA: You are welcome. We have not given you the smoke and everything here today. Here is to tell you, you have to quit.

> EREFE BUBEMI: Yes, sir.

> T. B. JOSHUA: Are you ready to quit?

> EREFE BUBEMI: [kneeling] Yes sir. I surrender.

Erefe Bubemi reappeared some two weeks later. A prayer had made the difference. She wanted to thank Prophet T. B. Joshua for the deliverance from her worldly ways. Beside her were her three children whom she had previously abandoned. Her mother was also there.

Remarkably, this was the first time she was in the presence of her mother and children in five years. The mother had seen her on Emmanuel TV when Prophet T. B. Joshua called her out. She was both happy and shocked by the story that unfolded.

Erefe could only say that frustration had driven her to prostitution. She realized that she had not been reasoning well. After prayer she had found peace.

"No more worry, no more urge of drinking, no more urge of smoking, no more urge to get men that will pay money for sleeping with them," she said. "I am not going back to prostitution." The church gave the family a cash gift of one hundred fifty thousand naira.

CHAPTER 6

WORLD PROPHECIES

The year 2020 opened with a list of world prophecies from T. B. Joshua.[1] Prophecy number eleven included the following intriguing words: "Pray for unity and understanding among the [British] Royal family, because of what I am seeing."

That was Sunday, January 5, 2020. On Wednesday, January 8, the news broke that the Duke and Duchess of Sussex had issued a statement that they were relinquishing their role as senior members of the British Royal family. They would be working to become financially independent.

The announcement shook the royal family.[2] Matters escalated when the Duke and Duchess' gave a sensational interview with American talk show host, Oprah Winfrey. The episode attracted a massive UK audience of 11.1 million. The Associated Press estimated the world audience to be in excess of fifty million. Senior royals at Buckingham palace were reported to be engaged in crisis talks.[3]

Another prophecy was COVID-19 related. "Many sicknesses and diseases that leaders have been treating privately will surface this year," he said.

He warned that 2020 would "be a year of humility" and "the Lord will humble us with our challenges."[4] Following the outbreak of the COVID-19 pandemic, he drew attention to a statement by US National Security Adviser Robert O'Brien which blamed China for covering up the outbreak, costing the world community two months of response time.

T. B. Joshua has made other significant prophecies that continue to unfold. They touch on the current economic challenges, and the problems with air travel. In this chapter I provide case studies of two important world prophecies issued by T. B. Joshua.

The first one concerns the Middle East, Syria, and the rise of the Islamic State of Iraq and the Levant, also known as the Islamic State of Iraq and Syria (ISIS). There was no attention paid to the prophecy. The world is the worse for it.

The second one focuses on the surprise Nigerian election that brought the opposition candidate Muhammadu Buhari of the All Progressives Congress (APC) to power. Incumbent President Goodluck Jonathan was the losing incumbent. The election marked the first time an incumbent president had lost re-election in Nigeria. The stunner was that the All Progressives Congress (APC) had only been formed on February 6, 2013, in anticipation of the 2015 elections.

T. B. Joshua had prophesied the emergence of this party for years before anyone knew what he was talking about. Later in the chapter, I will describe how T. B. Joshua was used by God to make a critical intervention in the transition from the Jonathan to the Buhari administration.

CASE 1: THE PROPHETIC WORD ON ISIS

Beginning in 2013, T. B. Joshua began to warn about an impending international crisis in Syria. Syria had been thrown out of the Arab League in 2011 over its violent response to opposition and dissent. As of 2020, the country has continued to be plagued with conflict.

Surrounding countries, especially Turkey and Iraq are embroiled in the conflict. Russia and the United States are also involved. T. B. Joshua repeatedly spoke on this matter on Emmanuel TV. During the live church service of September 1, 2013, he came back to the issue.[5] These were his words.

> I am here with a package message concerning the whole world about Syria. I told you about Iraq, and I told you about Egypt and I told you about Afghanistan. Syria now, if they go to war, I think this will humble the whole world. I will give you the details, how this will humble the whole world. It will not stop there. It will affect all its neighbors. Turkey should also be ready. For many years, there will be no peace in that region.
>
> If they are killing people in Syria, we should use other methods.

Whatever we can do now to not use sword to fight sword. I am just telling you what I am looking at, what I am seeing after the war. It is true you will succeed in crushing the whole thing there. But the whole region there—not one country, not two countries, not three countries, not four countries, not six countries—will not have peace for many years.

Do you know what is going to happen? Let me tell you what is going to happen. When the attack starts, the people you want to attack will run to neighboring countries. It is innocent people that will suffer there. Those who run to other countries will start trouble in those neighboring countries. They have visas, they can stay in all those countries we are talking about. What we are going to lose is bigger than what we gain.

The answer is whatever we can do now to appeal to the Arab League to come together and talk to our brother, the Syrian President, and make him part of the Arab League and begin the talks there. We gain more in doing that than by attacking. The man has already been removed from the Arab League. Let them call him. He is their brother.

On 17th August 2014, Prophet T.B. gave a follow-up message.[6] This was more specific about the Islamic State of Iraq and Syria (ISIS). He gave a warning concerning a wealthy terrorist organization attracting people from around the world and training them for war. He warned that trained recruits had already started returning to their countries as insurgents. The following is an edited transcript of the message.

I say this year is the year of crossing the bridge. Are you not seeing the bridge now? Crossing the bridge means a tough year. Very, very tough year. In January, I was telling you that there are some groups, and they are very rich. They will start a war. Money will not be their problem. It will be difficult to call them militants. They have what it takes—anything.

They have scientists among them. Professional gurus. Different countries will join them. You will find many countries signing up for that organization. I said it in January. Are you not seeing them now? Are you not seeing them in Iraq? There is no country that does not belong to that organization. They have split to different nations now. If each country belongs to that organization, any time they can go back to their country, and they can blow whatever plane they want there.

It's not an issue of don't let this country enter my country. It's your own countrymen that will do the job. I said it first week of January that there will be an organization and they will be so rich. And this organization will contain different people, different countries. As I am talking now, many of them have gone back to their countries.

It will be the most dangerous and sensitive war. It's like you are fighting your children, not another country. It's your citizens. They are well trained. The little time they spent in Iraq is enough for them to do anything, anywhere they go. It is time to be vigilant. Vigilant. It means there will be attacks of all kinds. Aircraft.

It is an impression that when it happens, it will not be some little thing. It will be something that once this happens, it will shake the whole world. Some of them signed for sick leave. Leave of one year, and you don't know where they went to. They went for holiday, but they are in Iraq for training for war. They will come back to the job they are doing in your country again to sign back as a spy. We continue to pray for the nations all over the world.

ISIS attracted global attention in 2014 after capturing territory in Iraq and taking a number of key cities. The organization soon became known for gross human rights abuses and war crimes. It spread rapidly, gaining fanatical adherents across the world and was reportedly operational in some eighteen countries at the end of 2015. At its peak, it was reported to have assets in excess of US $1 billion and an army of some thirty thousand fighters.[7] Adherents were drawn from across the world, including the United Kingdom, Belgium, the United States, and France. As 2020 began, the problem remained unresolved.[8]

CASE 2: THE 2015 NIGERIAN ELECTION

Nigeria held general elections on March 28 and 29, 2015. The incumbent president, Goodluck Jonathan, was seeking a second term. His People's

Democratic Party (PDP) had won every Presidential election between 1999 and 2011. The opposition candidate Muhammadu Buhari of the All Progressives Congress (APC) won the presidential election by more than 2.5 million votes.

The APC had been formed as an alliance of four opposition parties, the Action Congress of Nigeria, the Congress for Progressive Change, the All Nigeria Peoples Party, and the All Progressives Grand Alliance. The APC was only formed on February 6, 2013, in anticipation of the 2015 elections.

President Goodluck Jonathan conceded defeat on March 31 before the results from all thirty-six states had been announced. This was the first time in Nigeria's political history that an opposition political party had won an election and unseated a governing party in a peaceful transition.

Beginning in 2010, Prophet T.B. Joshua had been speaking about a new political party that would rise to challenge the ruling party within Nigeria and bring it to its knees.[9] The first message was on April 18, 2010. Prophet T. B. Joshua said, "In your country here, pray because I am seeing a party rise and challenging the super party of your country."

This was quite intriguing, given the dominance of the ruling party in 2010, and the fact that the APC was three years from being formed. Nobody knew what T. B. Joshua was talking about. He repeated the message several times including on January 19, 2013, and February 16, 2014.

Following the elections, T. B. Joshua spoke extensively about this prophecy and more generally about the prophetic ministry. The account is intriguing. I will limit myself to what he said about the Nigerian elections and how the outgoing president had come to concede in the face of severe pressure to reject the result from within his party.

T. B. Joshua talked about the revelation he had received about the president and his future prior to the election.

> I will tell you the reason why I said this. Six weeks before the election, I was praying because I was concerned about a dark cloud [over Nigeria]. The cloud was so dark. I heard a voice, and the cloud came upon me. "Right now, when you leave here, this message should be delivered to your president. Whatever the outcome of this election, his regime has come to an end. He should accept to save a million souls."

T. B. Joshua was able to establish contact with the president by phone. The president dispatched a top aide to the SCOAN. T. B. Joshua insisted that he should attend the service so that he would have a record of the visit. The message was duly delivered. On the last day of the election, T. B. Joshua called the president. He said to him, "Your excellency, all you need to say is 'thank you Jesus' when there seems to be nothing to be thankful for."

On that same day, it was announced that Jonathan had conceded. Goodluck Jonathan's concession was widely acclaimed. It was immediately recognized that this was a historic moment. Below is a partial transcript of how Will Ross and Marco Werman of the BBC reported the result. [10]

> MARCO WERMAN: Now to the history that was made in Nigeria today. President Goodluck Jonathan has officially conceded his defeat in the election that was held over the weekend, which means there will be a peaceful democratic transfer of power in Nigeria. That is the historic part, as my BBC colleague Will Ross told me from Lagos.

> WILL ROSS: This is a first for Nigeria and a hugely significant moment. Never before has a sitting president been voted out, and the fact that we hear President Goodluck Jonathan phoned the opposition's Muhammadu Buhari to congratulate him is a massive moment for Nigeria, and everybody hopes that it will calm down the tension. This country has been extremely tense over the last few months with both parties really fighting very hard with extraordinary amounts of money spent to win.

> It was a fairly close contest although it was very clear over the last twelve hours or so that President Goodluck Jonathan was going to struggle to narrow the gap after the former military ruler, General Buhari, opened up quite a considerable lead. But it does seem to be a sign of deepening democracy when you look back at all the coups that have taken place over the years, as well as so many rigged elections. This is a sign that you can vote out an unpopular government.

On this occasion Prophet T. B. Joshua shared some details about his prophetic ministry, the persecution he has faced, and the national and international events God had called him to act on. It was but a glimpse, but quite instructive. He explained how he hears from God in these words.

The way you read your newspaper is the way I hear God. When God speaks to me, I still want to ask, "My God, I can't hear you clearly." When I hear something, I will still ask again. If I am not clear, I will ask again. And I also want to pray whether there is someone out there that can change that message of God. I have been at it for a long time. I am an instrument to be used. A material that will not cost you any money.

That shows that this small boy, called T. B. Joshua, whom God is using to speak, if he speaks a word, and all of us take it, we capture Satan and his evil people. But because the man is living at Ikotun-Egbe, and we don't need a dictionary to understand his English—it's such elementary English—we don't think it is God that is speaking through him. And at the same time, he is not one of us. God did not inform us before he was anointed. God is supposed to tell us that he wants to anoint this small, rustic boy. We would have advised God that this is not the kind of boy you should anoint.[11]

CHAPTER 7

THE GOD OF MIRACLES

In June 2020 as the world reeled from the Covid-19 attack, the Synagogue Church of All Nations broadcast a healing episode. The case was that of Dr. Kameni Pierre, a Cameroonian gynecologist and obstetrician who had contracted the virus and was in quarantine. He reached out to the SCOAN for prayer. The healing prayer was broadcast.

The results were immediate. Dr. Kameni Pierre was shown to have been healed.[1] The results of tests before and after were proved the result. The story attracted wide attention across the world. World Health Organization Director-General, Dr. Tedros Ghebreyesus, and WHO Executive Director of Health Emergencies, Dr Michael Ryan were questioned about the miracle by Cameroonian journalist Simon Ateba during an interactive media session on Wednesday, July 1. According to news reports, Dr. Ryan affirmed the readiness of WHO to work with faith-based organizations like SCOAN to eradicate COVID-19.

Dr. Ghebreyesus is quoted as concurring.

"We know many religious leaders who would really advise their followers to follow their faith and at the same time use science," he said. "The two do not contradict; they go together…. We will call on all religious leaders to be in this fight and save lives."

T. B. Joshua has affirmed this point. This is quite clear in his published prayer of April 19, 2020, when he prayed, "For those on the sickbed, may our doctors, nurses, caregivers sense the presence of God, in the name of Jesus Christ."

The prayer affirms the role of medicine for the improvement of livelihoods. There are good reasons for this. First, even as faith leaders recognize that the public health challenges require all parties to do their part especially in a pandemic.

A second point is that miracles in the Church serve a larger purpose beyond physical healings. The Dutch philosopher and theologian, Willem J. Ouweneel, who is acquainted with the work of T. B. Joshua has expressed this point quite well. Miracles serve to point people to God and to spiritual salvation.

> God can give five thousand people bread via the baker as well as via Jesus. The enormous difference is that the baker route does not give a powerful witness, but that of Jesus does. When we receive bread from the baker or healing via a doctor, we are grateful to God. But when five thousand people all receive food from five loaves via a servant of God or people on whom the medical doctors have given up are healed via a healing service, a powerful witness is present that tells us that God is present here in a special way.[2]

T. B. Joshua has also spoken about the importance of miracles in the life of the Church. "If millions are to believe, they must see proof that Jesus Christ is the same yesterday, today and forever," he has said.

"Jesus performed many other signs in the presence of his disciples, which are not recorded in this book," wrote the apostle John. "But these are written that you may believe that Jesus is the Messiah, the Son of God, and that by believing you may have life in his name." (John 20:30-31 [NIV])

That is the mission of the Synagogue Church of All Nations. "You are healed for the salvation of your soul," T. B. Joshua has said.[3]

I should also point out that many medical personnel, other than Dr. Kameni Pierre of Cameroon, have turned to the SCOAN for help when they could not get relief from hospitals. Among them are Dr. Blossom Gwavu from South Africa[4] (chronic knee injury, see picture); Dr. James King Oshiorenua from Nigeria (depression, delusion, and suicidal); Dr. Gerrie de Haas from South Africa[5] (deafness); Dr. Irma Bendar from Russia[6] (writer's spasm); and Dr. Frank Voado from the United States[7] (lumbar spondylosis). T. B. Joshua has a high regard for medical personnel. "Doctors treat and God heals," he has often said.

Doctors who have received healing have often been surprised to see their prayers answered. One such case occurred on March 16, 2020. In this case, God used the medium of Living Water from the church. This was the case of

6. Dr Gwavu and her husband testify at the SCOAN

a medical doctor suffering from diabetes type I for five years. He was healed using the medium of water. T. B. Joshua has often used anointed water as a medium for healing and deliverance. The doctor was asked for his advice as a medical doctor.

> I didn't believe that God can do all these miracles, but today is very shocking. What will I say? I believe that God can perform miracles through water. Ordinary water. Living Water. It's not just ordinary. The anointing is there. Water is only a compound, hydrogen and oxygen. With this same water, He has healed me. Thank you, Jesus! Thank you, Jesus!

Prophet T. B. Joshua has sometimes referred cases to medical practitioners. One case was that of a young boy who turned up for help at the SCOAN with a severe neck injury.[8] A gang of armed robbers had attacked his family, slit his throat, and left him in a pool of blood, presuming he was dead. The rest of his family were murdered. T. B. Joshua spent US $9,000 to airlift the boy to South Africa for specialist surgery. He was fully restored and has continued to be cared for by the ministry.

In a related case, the ministry paid for the airlifting and surgery of a security guard who had been shot during a bank robbery. He received groin surgery in India.

During a pastors' conference held in the Dominican Republic in November 2017, Prophet T. B. Joshua called out a woman from the audience whom he said was trying to avoid surgery. He asked her to come forward.

"I want to counsel you," he said. "You will still go for the operation. It will come out successfully. God will lead the doctor to do it."

The woman reluctantly came forward and confirmed the story. She was Rossana Marte from Miami, Florida. She had a fibroid the size of her head. Months later, she visited the SCOAN where she shared the story of a very successful surgery. She had fully recovered and her womb had been saved.

The case of Rossana Marte and the other examples I have shared provide some clarity on T. B. Joshua's perspective. He has seen his work and that of health care providers as complementary and not as tension. The work at the SCOAN has served to fill in the gaps in health care, in addition to providing critical testimonies of the love and power of the living God. In that regard, it is practically impossible to keep track of the number of healings that have occurred at the church. Six cases are shared to provide a deeper understanding of the healing ministry.

CASE 1: JUDE ORAKA IS HEALED OF A SKIN DISEASE

Jude Oraka showed up at the SCOAN with a life-threatening disease. The case, which I originally viewed live, has now been archived by Emmanuel TV and includes a commentary.[9] The story opens with the camera zooming in from a full body shot then to a medium shot of a man sitting on a chair. He is separated from others, his body quivering in the sunshine and wearing nothing but a pair of shorts. A close-up shot reveals horrendous skin damage.

> NARRATOR: A shocking condition brought this man to the Synagogue Church of All Nations, his body riddled with sickness. Right from the crown of his head, his entire body has been engulfed in a plague, shattering his skin into scale-like fragments. There is not a hair left on his head as the frightening sickness has completely destroyed the skin. From his head, the disease rages across his body, damaging every inch and rendering his arms useless. The skin flakes and peels horribly all the way down his arms to his fingers. Not one inch of his skin has been left unaffected.

JUDE ORAKA: [barely able to speak] My name is Jude Oraka. I come from Anambra State [Nigeria]. My age is thirty-nine years.

T. B. JOSHUA: Watch your screen. That will help your faith. Look at the case here. It is a mysterious issue. I never knew how he came here because I don't know the kind of vehicle that would convey this man here. So, let him get free and go.

JUDE'S SISTER: Man of God, help my brother. He has skin disease for the past six years. We have taken him all over. There is no solution. Neither the herbalist's homes or hospitals have provided any solution. [10]

T. B. JOSHUA: Ok, let's hear from your brother. What is your problem? Can you talk?

T. B. JOSHUA: [Oraka is struggling to talk] It seems he cannot talk. As you see his appearance, so it is on the inside. Are you ready to accept Jesus as your Lord and Savior?

JUDE ORAKA: Yes.

T. B. JOSHUA: Thank you. I command that disease, that infirmity in your body, in the name of Jesus Christ. I command that infirmity out! Begin to vomit it out! [11]

T. B. JOSHUA: [T. B. Joshua watches the man intently for about fifteen seconds, then he speaks again] I say to you disease, you can hear me. Come out of this man's life! In the name of Jesus, come out! Out!

T. B. JOSHUA: [the man begins to shake uncontrollably and bends forward to throw up something white and foamy] You can see what the Name of Jesus can do. Out! I say out, in the Name of Jesus! It must come out because the name Jesus is given to cast out demons and to speak to disease. We have dominion over all disease, all affliction, infirmity, trouble, and the challenges of your life.

T. B. JOSHUA: [the man continues to throw up] It's poison. He drank poison. Look here! In the Name of Jesus, stand up! He is free.

That was it. The man wandered away with his sister, walking unsteadily. The man returned later, fully restored, from head to toe. The before and after comparison was stunning. The congregation was moved to stand up for a sustained applause.

CASE 2: DAVID OGEN
FROM THE UNITED KINGDOM

Mr. David Ogen, who was suffering from colon cancer, came to the SCOAN with his wife. The doctors had put Ogen on chemotherapy for five weeks, every day of the week. The wife was alarmed. "Why are you on chemotherapy for 5 days a week? They want to kill you," she asked of him.

He was stooling blood uncontrollably. His condition became so severe that he had stopped working. His wife also stopped working to take care of him, putting the family's livelihood in jeopardy. His case is more fully presented in archival video for which I have provided a link.[12]

The doctors had proposed a high-risk surgery but the prognosis was very bleak. Ogen opted to go to the SCOAN. He received the briefest of touches from T. B. Joshua who did not even speak to him. Humanly speaking, the level of attention did not measure up to the seriousness of the case. But something

7. David Ogen tells of his cancer healing

did happen. The cancer left his body. Ogen came back a year later with the testimony. He was accompanied by his wife and a little baby.

During the testimony, Ogen and his wife recounted how the doctors had been incredulous when he reported that he was healed. They conducted comprehensive tests, three in all. The tests confirmed that the cancer was completely gone. Ogen brought all the reports and images for the church audience to see.

CASE 3: MRS. RAUNA KAKEHONGO OF NAMIBIA HEALED OF CANCER.

The second cancer case is that of twenty-nine-year-old Rauna Kakehongo, a wife and mother, who came from Namibia. She had stage 4 lymphoma (a blood cancer). Stage 4 is the last stage of cancer. Death was on her doorstep.[13]

All medical options had been exhausted, including chemotherapy and surgery. She brought the many medications that she was taking to manage the pain and suffering. They included steroids, pain killers and antibiotics. Her body was numb and she was struggling to sit. She had a letter from her life insurance company that granted here a waiver to immediately receive her death benefits in order to prepare for her funeral. This and other related documents are part of her videotaped testimony.

Kakehongo's hopes were raised when she started watching Emmanuel TV. Even against the advice of her doctor, she was determined to visit and she was healed. As in the case of Ogen, the encounter with T. B. Joshua was split second.

Rauna Kakehongo visited the SCOAN twice after her healing. She was there a year after the healing, and again four years later. Each time, she testified publicly. She recounted how on her first return home, the doctors were stunned and incredulous about her story. She was put through four comprehensive tests including one in South Africa, using the most advanced procedures. All tests confirmed her perfect health. She found herself becoming a medical curiosity. Annual medical reviews had continued to show perfect health.

In her final visit she recounted the agony of her first trip to the SCOAN. "I was here without hope. I was here looking for the last blessing before my departure to my last home. But by the grace of God, I am here today in your midst. Thank you, God, for Prophet T. B. Joshua's life."

When asked to give her advice to others, she simply said, "Jesus died on the cross for us. So, apply your faith."

8. Rauna Kakehongo rejoices in her healing

There are many other cases of cancer healings. Arceli Arzate Cedillo from Mexico City, Mexico suffered from lung and colon cancer and was healed at the Mexico Crusade, and Edith Afesume was healed of ovarian cancer.[14] I will now turn to two cases of HIV/ADS.

CASE 4: MR. AND MRS. NWOYE HEALED OF HIV/AIDS

Davidson Nwoye was forty-two years old when he showed up at the SCOAN with his wife. Both confessed to living promiscuous and adulterous lives that had led to deadly infections. The symptoms included acute bodily pains, bodily rashes and itches, urinary tract pains, and headache. His tearful wife was only twenty-six years old. A good Samaritan suggested the SCOAN, and they came out of desperation.

T. B. Joshua stretched his hand out, and something happened. They showed up fourteen years later, looking older, and full of life and joy.[15] They were keen to share their story. They had each been tested twice following the original visit. They confessed that the second tests were to dispel their doubts. They brought the results of all the tests. They were also keen to counsel others.

"Viewers all over the world, my advice is that HIV/AIDS is real. Stop jumping from one person or place to another. If you are married, stick to your wife …Our own role is to go and sin no more so that the blessing we have received will remain permanent in our lives," said Davidson Nwoye.

CASE 5: MRS. NKACHUKWU ORAKWUE ODELE RETURNS AFTER TWELVE YEARS TO SHARE HER TESTIMONY.

Nkachukwu Odele originally visited the SCOAN as an unmarried woman suffering from an HIV/AIDS infection. She returned twelve years later, as a married woman, to share her testimony. She brought all her reports to prove that she had contracted the sickness and that she was now free of the disease (her documentation is part of her videotaped testimony).

Nkachukwu Odele was moved to come back after reading an article that claimed there was no record of anyone healed of HIV /AIDS at the SCOAN. She was determined to come back and dispel the falsehood.

"People should not be believing lies from the internet and other sources. Look at me, I am a living testimony," she said.

She knew of many others besides herself who had receive healing at the SCOAN.

"We call each other, and we are all comfortably ok," she said. "Some are married with children. They no longer experience the symptoms, and they give glory to God."

She recounted the instructions T. B. Joshua had given them to maintain their healing. He had said, "Go and sin no more."

I will conclude with the story of Mrs. Rosemary Imma from Nigeria.

CASE 6: MRS. ROSEMARY IMMA

Mrs. Imma's claim to fame is that she was featured in an internationally published story by Rowan Moore Gerety.[16] I will say more about this in chapter 10.

Mrs. Imma came to the SCOAN overnight with a ruptured nasal artery. Doctors had failed to stop the bleeding. This was a clear emergency.[17] A pre-interview was conducted before Rosemary Imma was placed on the prayer line. Her husband recounted how they had been at the hospital for days and the problem was unresolved. As he spoke, blood started gushing out through her nose and mouth. It was a most disturbing and unnerving sight.[18]

When T. B. Joshua appeared, he was stunned by the sight of the woman. "You need to see what I am looking at. I want you to look. Watch your screen. Oh, my God!" he said.

In the next fleeting moment, T. B. Joshua raised his hand with a shout. "Receive your healing in the name of Jesus Christ. Thank you, Lord. Stand up!" Waving her up, T. B. Joshua then said, "She is free."

Mrs. Imma stood up, holding her bloodied bowl. "Thank you, Jesus. I'm free."

By then T. B. Joshua had moved on.

Archival video shows that Mrs. Imma was indeed healed. She joyfully returned the following week to share her miracle. On her return, she was accompanied by two brothers and her husband, who were all eager to share the story.

She said the bleeding had lasted eight days. The medical personnel could not

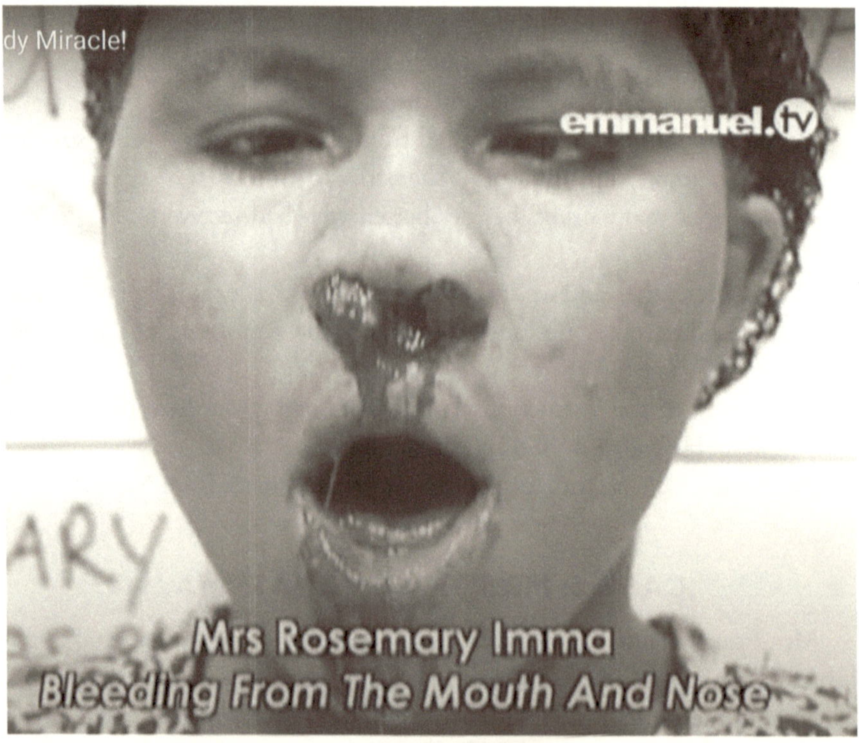

9. Rosemary Imma rushed to the SCOAN for healing

stop the blood flow and only sustained her life through massive blood transfusions. For some reason, the hospital discharged her without stopping the bleeding. Her life was clearly in danger. In desperation, the family rushed to the SCOAN, traveling through the night.

According to her, she felt a change when T. B. Joshua said, "Receive your healing!"

She felt the bleeding stopping "just like that." During her testimony, it was also revealed that she was eight months pregnant and the bleeding had threatened the life of the baby.

The SCOAN maintained contact with Mrs. Rosemary Imma and her family. She came back a third time, this time with her baby. Her entourage was made up of her husband, her mother-in-law, her sister-in-law, and her brother-in-law. They came to give thanks, highlighting the significance of the healing in their family life.

LET YOUR FAITH BE LIFTED UP

T. B. Joshua does not say that this generation necessarily lacks faith. Rather, he emphasizes the importance of growing one's faith and raising expectations of what God can do. Faith grows spontaneously as we witness the grace and power of God through reading and believing the Word as well as hearing testimonies. As our trust in God grows, He is able to accomplish more in our lives. He uses the metaphor of faith as a "heavenly currency."[19]

> Faith is a heavenly currency we use to purchase, to receive heavenly blessings. When you get to the market, you begin to negotiate. How much is this? Five naira. You have three naira. That money is not enough. That does not mean you don't have money. What you need is to go back and get more money. So, in the same vein, when you say, "Heal me, heal me," and you are not healed, that does not mean you don't have faith. It is only the measure of faith to purchase that healing you don't have.

In his message, T. B. Joshua elaborated on the challenges that people face when their prayers are not answered.

> If you cannot receive today, it does not mean you don't have faith. You probably don't have the measure of faith you need. Don't

condemn yourself. That does not mean you are not a child of God. You are still a child of God. When you ask from God and you do not receive, the devil will come in and say, "Can you see, you are not a child of God."

Your mind will begin to be disturbed. "If I am a child of God, God should give me what I ask for. I have been at it for many years now. I keep asking God, "give me, give me," but others are receiving, and I am not receiving."

When you offer prayer, the devil will come to you and say, "Can you see you are not a child of God. If you are a child of God, you should receive it now." You probably do not have the degree, the measure of faith to receive that healing. That does not make you an unbeliever. You just need to continue to press on, keep growing in faith to receive what you need from God. Hearing and obeying the Word of God grows your faith.

CHAPTER 8

EMMANUEL TV

Changing Lives, Changing Nations, and Changing the World

Emmanuel TV was inaugurated on March 8, 2006. It emerged out of the heat of persecution when T. B. Joshua was banned from broadcasting on the national broadcasting network.[1] It is both a television broadcast network and a charity. Surprisingly, the name 'Emmanuel TV' was not T. B. Joshua's first choice. The name was given to him by God through revelation. He had other ideas.

Emmanuel TV seemed too much of a mouthful when compared to established networks such as BBC, CNN, or ABC. But God prevailed. The name comes from Matthew 1:23 ("The virgin will conceive and give birth to a son, and they will call him Immanuel"), which means "God with us." Emmanuel TV has been used by God to change lives and situations across the world. In this chapter, I present selected examples of how the Emmanuel TV charity has been used to meet the needs of individuals and communities across the world. Below are examples of this good work.

CASE 1: EMMANUEL TV COMES TO THE RESCUE OF FREDDIE FROM LIMA, PERU.

In 2016, T. B. Joshua held a crusade in Lima, Peru. Among those who came was Freddie, a forty-three-year-old alcoholic, a problem that had plagued him for twenty-two years. He had been imprisoned twice. Freddie was homeless and spent his nights in a local park. His ate from rubbish bins and sometimes he resorted to theft. He was a picture of destitution when he turned up at the Estadio Monumental Stadium. An estimated one hundred thousand people came to the two-day event. God had an appointment with Freddie. He found his deliverance through a prayer from T. B. Joshua.[2] The urge to drink completely left him.

10. Freddie shows the places where he has lived

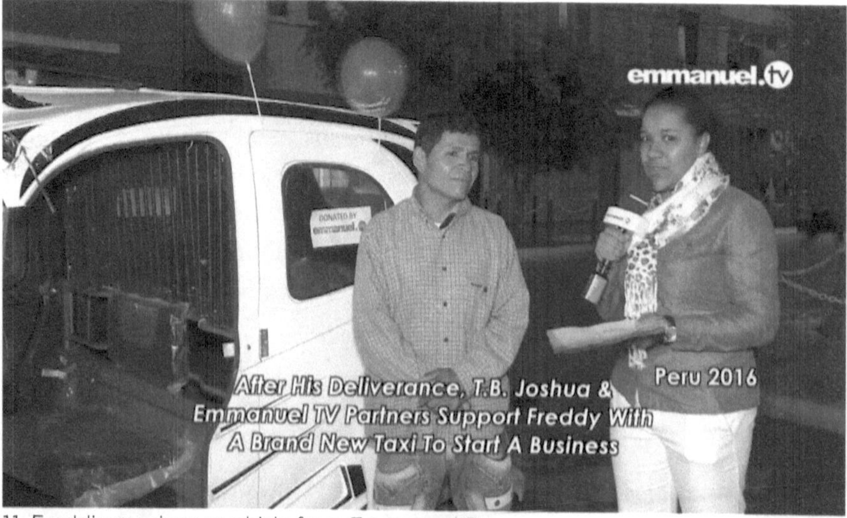

11. Freddie receives a vehicle from Emmanuel TV

An Emmanuel TV team followed up with Freddie after the crusade. The team was moved to purchase an apartment for him and furnished it. Overjoyed Freddie shed tears when he saw his new home. "I thank God with all my heart," he said.

Before his problems started, Freddie had been a taxi driver. The ministry saw an opportunity to help him restart his life. A brand-new vehicle was purchased for him to start a taxi business.

CASE 2: A DESTITUTE WIDOWER IS COMFORTED

Mr. Ezekiel Ayodeji, a forty-five-year-old man, appeared at the SCOAN in search of help. He was disabled, a widower, and a father of three. His source of income, a shop, had burned down, his children had been sent away from school, and he was now homeless. The family was completely destitute. T. B. Joshua was moved to comment.

> You have listened to that. There are many people like this in your community. These are the people that make your money useless because it has meaning when you spend it on these people. Money becomes a curse when we are not spending it on the needy.

He directed that 300,000 naira should be given to the man for immediate relief. The Emmanuel TV charity provided support to send the children back to school, as well as accommodation. The family were also given six bags of rice. Ezekiel Ayodeji was also presented with a new car.

The story took a strange turn the following week. The man came back and reported that he had acquired a plot of land. But he had also given his pastor 30,000 naira (10 percent of his SCOAN gift), as a tithe. He now had 50,000 naira left. He was not a member of the Synagogue Church of All Nations and he worshipped at another church.

T. B. Joshua was not happy with the 30,000 naira tithe. "I am going to return that 30,000 naira to you now," he said. "There are many areas where you can render your service to the ministry. But financially, you are not strong." He said the man could pay the tithe later, when he had secured his financial position. "You should serve God in that church. It is a good church."

CASE 3: A THIRTEEN-YEAR-OLD FINDS RELIEF

Miracle Khubai was thirteen years old when she visited the SCOAN. Hers was a sad story. She had a musculoskeletal condition resulting from a horrendous flogging by a teacher at her school. Her movements were severely curtailed. "When my mom is not there, I cannot get to the toilet, and I will mess myself up on the bed," the girl said. She was not able to go to school. "I feel heartbroken and sad because this has affected my life."

She only sat with difficulty and was in constant pain. A letter from the New Life Medical Center in Botswana dated January 26, 2017, confirmed her condition. The family had also sought medical help in South Africa but found no relief.

Prophet T. B. Joshua was clearly touched by the case. He prayed for the mother, and then the girl. She immediately got up and was able to walk. "Thank you, Jesus. I can walk!" the little girl tearfully exclaimed.

After the healing, the family received a handsome gift of US$2,000 from Emmanuel TV charity. The mother was very touched. She recounted how the church had housed and fed them during their stay at no charge. There was another surprise for the family. The Emmanuel TV charity granted the little girl a scholarship to cover the cost of her education up to university level.

CASE 4: LIBYAN DEPORTEES

The economic challenges in many parts of Africa have compelled young people to attempt illegal entry into Europe. They have followed the deadliest route on Earth which cuts through the Sahara Desert, going through Libya and other countries. Libya has been particularly dangerous. Vicious militias and other opportunistic gangs have preyed on the migrants. Many have been robbed and killed. Others have been arrested, detained, and deported back to Nigeria. Those who make it to the sea face a perilous crossing in overcrowded and unsafe boats. Many have perished on the seas.[3]

On the evening of June 16, 2016, a total of one hundred and six Nigerian deportees arrived at the SCOAN in search of help. This was one of many groups of deportees that have come to the SCOAN in search of help. The returnees told horrific stories of torture, rape, forced labor, human trafficking, slavery, and death.

Prior to the arrival of the group at the SCOAN, Nima Elbagir, the award-winning senior international correspondent for CNN, had covered the story of these people from deep inside Libya. The report provided proof of their story, including evidence of slave auctioning. Featured in that story was Victory Imasuen, who was part of the group.

Imasuen was from Edo, Nigeria. His father had died when he was eleven, leaving behind a wife and six children. He worked as a barber but was not making enough money to meet the needs. A customer suggested that he go to Europe and set himself as a barber. He would help him for a fee of 340,000 naira. Imasuen paid part of the fee and promised the balance when he got to Europe. To cross the desert, he found himself stacked in a truck with thirty other people. There were fatal accidents on the way. Most of the group died. There were demands for payment that he and others could not meet. This is how he ended up being put up for sale as a slave. The ladies in their company were sold to prostitution rackets. A second attempt to cross into Europe failed. He was arrested. There were at least ten thousand other Nigerians in the Libyan prison. He was in prison when Nima Elbagir of CNN interviewed him.

Imasuen and other deportees were welcomed at the SCOAN. The Emmanuel TV charity initially provided a total of 1,200,000 naira to the group. An additional 200,000 naira was added later. As noted above, this was but one of the many such groups of Libyan deportees that have passed through the SCOAN.

The Emmanuel TV charity was being used by God to meet material needs. However, the concern went deeper than this. Prophet T. B. Joshua had come to understand that situations of pain, suffering, and extreme deprivation are sources of temptation. "When you are so poor, you will lose sense of judgment, sense of reason. You cannot reason well. You cannot say what is right and what is wrong. You can easily be deceived," he has said.[4]

The story of Imasuen and other deportees is an example. The case of Sifawo Okoro is as well.

CASE 5: SIFAWO OKORO'S EUROPEAN NIGHTMARE

Sifawo Okoro's face was a picture of sadness when she appeared at the SCOAN.[5] It is not clear what she expected, but she held deep secrets. When

Prophet T. B. Joshua spoke to her, he went to the source of her troubled life. She was too startled to respond coherently. The encounter was as follows:

> T. B. JOSHUA: I am seeing a man called Lawson.

> SIFAWO OKORO: [no response]

> T. B. JOSHUA: What you don't want people to know, when it happens, it will disappoint people who love you so much. It is a heavy load you cannot share with anyone.

> SIFAWO OKORO: [crying] Yes, it is true, sir.

It took her some time to finally say Lawson was "the man that took me to Europe for prostitution." She was prayed for. She later narrated how her sister had introduced her to this Lawson. It was said that he assisted young people to enter Europe illegally and secure jobs. Sifawo Okoro hoped to do menial work, perhaps, working in a bar, washing plates and glasses. But once in Europe, it emerged that Lawson's real business was the sex trade.

> SIFAWO OKORO: When we got there, he told me that I should wear sexy clothes and that I was going to the streets to work. I said, "No. I can't do the street work. You told me I was going to work in bars, wash plates and glasses. Why are you sending me to go and work in the street?" He said I should go into the street and work because I have to pay back the money. I now said, "I don't have any options. I had to go." When I went into the streets in the night six men took me. I brought 120 euros.

She had to pay Lawson a staggering 50,000 euros and she did. By the time she was through with the payment, she was very sick. She needed surgery and lost a kidney.

> T. B. JOSHUA: They removed your kidney?

> SIFAWO OKORO: Yes, sir.

> T. B. JOSHUA: You have one kidney?

> SIFAWO OKORO: Yes, sir.

T. B. JOSHUA: How did you go to Europe?

SIFAWO OKORO: My elder sister called me and told me about a man that took girls to Europe.

T. B. JOSHUA: It's alright. A man took girls to Europe. To dance? To study? To a job? Or to do what? A man you do not know. He wants to give you scholarship to Europe? So, you, you played a role in destroying your life. It's a lesson to everyone. It is not where you are, but what you are. No continent can change you if you are not ready to change.

Sifawo Okoro was allowed to stay at the church for some weeks receiving support and counseling. By the time she left, she was a transformed woman, full of joy, rejoicing in her renewed confidence and restoration.

"Everything about me has changed," she said beaming with joy. "I am a new person in Christ."

She received a gift of money from the Emmanuel TV charity to help her restart her life.

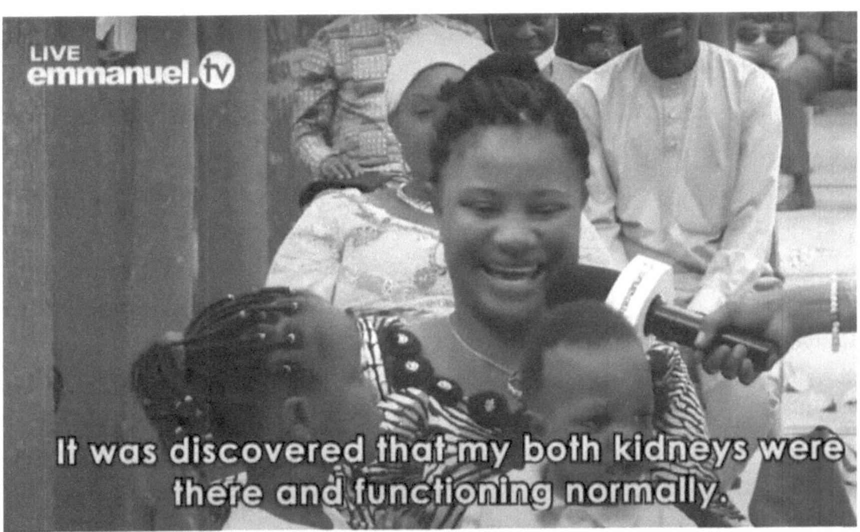

12. Okoro: "You can see me now, everything has changed!

On April 24, 2021, Okoro reappeared at the Synagogue Church of All Nations.[6] She was now married with two children. "I am so happy today. For

God changed my life, for giving me a new life again. Thank you, Jesus. Thank you, the God of Prophet T. B. Joshua."

She recounted her bad life and how she had lost the left kidney. Following prayers, she was completely healed. She was shocked when the doctor reported that her left kidney was normal. "You can see me now, everything has changed! The doctor even said I could not have a child. But God blessed me with a wonderful husband and two children. A boy and a girl. Thank you, Jesus."

BEYOND COLOR, CREED OR BACKGROUND

The Emmanuel TV charity makes no distinctions between people based on race, ethnicity, religion, or origin. In 2103, T. B. Joshua received a prestigious merit award as an Ambassador of Peace from the Arewa Youth Forum, which is a Nigerian Muslim youth organization.[7] The National Director of Public Affairs for the Arewa Youth Forum, Bello Abdulhamid, said the presentation was because of the love that T. B. Joshua always demonstrated irrespective of race, religion, creed or ethnicity.

The Emmanuel TV charity has covered many areas including job creation and employment, deportee resettlement, stranded persons, persons with disabilities, orphans, little people, widows, the elderly, education and scholarships, and the rehabilitation of gang members, political thugs, and prostitutes.

The ministry's scholarship program for students is extensive. The most high-profile cases include Harvard-educated lawyer Mary-Jean Nleya from Botswana whom T. B. Joshua began to support in the early stages of her university education.

Yinka Oduwole is an Oxford-educated scientist whom T. B. Joshua sponsored for all her graduate work at the University of London and Oxford University.

The geographic areas have included Ghana, Philippines, Haiti, UK, India, Israel, Mexico, Colombia, Namibia, Nigeria, Pakistan, Russia, South Africa, Ukraine, USA, Zimbabwe, Ecuador, Laos, and Indonesia.

In Colombia, the charity donated US$100,000 to the police to assist in crime fighting.

In Israel, charity donated kidney dialysis equipment to a hospital facility, and in the USA, Emmanuel TV has provided food packages to low-income families.

In Paraguay, God used the charity to rescue Mario Anibal Gimenez Ruiz, a

severely troubled transvestite. A prayer transformed him, restoring his true identity in Christ. The ministry paid over US $3,000 to reverse the breast implants
and provided him a new wardrobe of clothes.

The following are specific examples of large-scale work conducted by the
Emmanuel TV charity.

THE ECUADOR INITIATIVE

On April 16, 2016, a devastating 7.8 earthquake struck the nation of Ecuador. One of the places that was hit hardest was the indigenous community of
San Salvador de Los Chachis. T. B. Joshua was moved to assist. An Emmanuel
TV Ecuador Earthquake Relief Team was formed. Emmanuel TV chartered a
plane and dispatched some twenty tons of relief aid. The restoration of the Juan
Lorenzo Añapa Educational school became the focus of relief efforts. Located in
the rainforest, this was the main primary and secondary school in the area. The
restored school has modern facilities, including a fully equipped computer suite.

13. Prophet TB Joshua and his wife Evelyn are received by Ecuadorian generals

In 2017, Prophet T. B. Joshua and his wife Evelyn traveled to Ecuador to open
the reconstructed school. It turned out to be a grueling epic journey through the
dense tropical rainforest, on roads that were in some parts impassable.

When officially opening the school, T. B. Joshua proclaimed that it would be educating future leaders. Raul Pulupa Vera became the first fruit of that effort. In 2020 he commenced studies at the Pontifical Catholic University of Ecuador which is the top university in the country. He enrolled in the Agro-Industrial Engineering program and has been fully sponsored by Emmanuel TV.

HAITI INITIATIVE

On January 12, 2010, thousands of Haitians lost their lives, homes and families in a devastating earthquake. Emmanuel TV chartered two planes from Florida, USA to fly medical supplies and foodstuffs. T. B. Joshua also assembled and dispatched a team of medical doctors, nurses, engineers, evangelical and humanitarian workers. The team established Clinique Emmanuel which became the center of the SCOAN's relief efforts. The full scope the relief effort is described in the SCOAN publication, *Roadmap: Reaching Out To A Troubled World.*

A SCHOOL IN LAHORE, PAKISTAN

Emmanuel School in Lahore, Pakistan is one of the many international humanitarian charity projects undertaken by the ministry. In 2012, the ministry reported that construction of the school was completed. Since then, the school has provided top quality education to children who had never been in school.

LOW-INCOME AND ELDERLY COMMUNITIES IN THE USA

Under the banner, *Love always looks around, Love always searches to see who is in need,* Emmanuel TV charity has been active in the state of Ohio, USA. The effort is directed toward low-income neighborhoods, to the elderly and disabled, and youth. A fully stocked pantry has been set up. The items provided to the community include potatoes, bread, dry foods and meat. The meat is stored in refrigerators at an Emmanuel TV facility. Jeff Singleton, who is a local resident has expressed gratitude.

> We have the elderly, the disabled, people who are unemployed, the homeless, and people who are struggling, scraping finger to toe, trying to make it every day in life. Just doing what we can to survive. I

14. Ecuador earthquake relief: TB Joshua's visit was a test of grit and love

could never thank you enough, but T. B. Joshua, you are a blessing to us and many others. God bless you and for everything you do.

Eunice Thomas, a local widow has become an Emmanuel TV volunteer. She has spoken about the Emmanuel TV project.

> I am from Cincinnati, Ohio. People need you. It was a blessing that you guys came. There are a lot of people struggling like myself. Some people have no income, some are disabled, trying to get disability support. I am a widow also. There are a lot of elderly people and people with kids. There are a lot of people that work, but still can't make ends meet.
>
> A lot of people team up as one household or whatever to try to make ends meet. So, anything they can be helped with, they will be grateful. I appreciate it. Before you came, I was really depressed and didn't know what today or tomorrow was going to bring. When you came, it brightened me up. T. B. Joshua, thank you very much. If there is anything I can do beyond this, don't hesitate to contact me. I am available.

A backpack program has provided food items for each child to ensure that they have healthy food. The backpacks are refilled once a week. The children have also received a small regular cash gift. The message from T. B. Joshua is that they should stay in school and maintain a clear purpose for their lives.

SCOAN AND CHARITY WORK: A NEW FACE OF AFRICA

In July 2009, the American Women's Club (AWC) wrote a letter of appreciation to T. B. Joshua in appreciation of the support he had provided to repatriate a "distraught American lady who had come to the SCOAN seeking refuge."[8] Her circumstances are not quite clear, but she was reported to have found herself "held against her will after arriving two and a half years ago."

The SCOAN took action to provide support for her and paid for her repatriation to the United States. "Your support is truly appreciated," wrote Donna Blair, Honorary President (AWC), and Mary Walker (Executive Board member, AWC). "Your willingness to shelter her represents all that a church is meant to represent. Additionally, you cared to have someone follow her home to know the address. Then to have paid for her return trip home was far more than any of us expected." They concluded, "Pastor Joshua, you and your staff are very much cherished, we are aware you adjusted you schedule to accommodate the young lady and your efforts are not taken for granted."

This is but one instance of this type of support. In one well documented case, the ministry provided shelter and support to a Mongolian woman and mother of two who had fled from her marital home. The ministry attempted to reconcile the woman and her husband. When that failed, the Emmanuel TV charity paid for the repatriation of the woman to Mongolia, with her two children.[9] The repatriation package was US $7,000, of which $4,000 was for airfares, and $3,000 was a cash gift to support the woman to resettle in her country.

From the beginning, the SCOAN has projected a self-confident global image, not bound by national boundaries, nor by race, creed, or tradition. The ministry projects a new vision of Africa, quite different from the dependency commonly associated with the continent. When T. B. Joshua has traveled abroad for his crusades, he pays his way and takes no collection. In fact, he has donated to needy persons and communities.

The world was stunned when he paid for the rehabilitation of the Amphitheatre of Mount Precipice in Nazareth which was the venue of his June 2019 crusade. Prior to that, the venue was rundown, neglected, and covered with grass and weeds. Emmanuel TV brought in heavy earth moving equipment, construction teams and landscape designers and transformed the site. All for the glory of God.

People respond to such visionary and selfless leadership. T. B. Joshua has become a much beloved and trusted person. That bond of affection and trust is the secret to the resources he is able to command.

In 2008, the late Nigerian President, Umaru Musa Yar'Adua conferred the Officer of the Order of the Federal Republic (OFR) on T. B. Joshua in recognition of "outstanding virtues and appreciation of services" to the nation Nigeria. The citation highlighted his humanitarian efforts over twenty years and encouraged others "to learn from his lifestyle."

ANNUS HORRIBILIS

Annus horribilis' is a Latin phrase, meaning 'horrible year.' The year 2014 was a most horrible year for T. B. Joshua and the Synagogue Church of All Nations family. The year started with a big surprise when Prophet T. B. Joshua travelled to Cali, Colombia for a crusade. The turnout was in excess of one hundred thousand and the presence of God was stunning.

One lost count of the number of people who were healed and of those who were delivered from demonic oppression. The Emmanuel Television team made numerous follow-ups on the testimonies. The crusade ended with a pastors' conference and charity work in the community. In addition to other gifts, T. B. Joshua made a surprise donation of US $100,000 to the police in Cali.

News of the crusade was covered across the world. This was the first ever venture of the ministry into the Americas and the event caught the imagination of many believers. T. B. Joshua was flooded with invitations to continue with the tour in other South American countries. He briefly considered the offers, but God spoke to him and ordered him to immediately return to Lagos.

THE DARK CLOUD

When T. B. Joshua spoke to the congregation on his return, his message was uncharacteristically somber. My wife and I listened to the message on the live broadcast, and we were left uneasy. We had expected a bright account of the historic visit to Colombia. He did talk about that, but he was more preoccupied with the future. This is what T. B. Joshua said.[1]

I came back from Columbia. I wanted to travel from there to another country. But I came back home because there is a cloud that covers Nigeria. I want to witness how that cloud will dispel. Cloud means trouble.

Look at what is happening here. You will not see it on national TV, but if you learned that they bombed here, one of you will call CNN that they have bombed the SCOAN. All that is happening, you will never see it on the pages of national newspapers, or internationally. You will never see it—every good thing. But, if anything bad happens in front of the church, one of you Nigerians will be the one to make a call.

You are destroying your country, selling your country at nothing. It's a very painful thing. You are the ones destroying your country, you Nigerians. The image you are giving to your country is bad. You destroy your image. You say your nation is bad; everything is bad; the good is bad. I am telling you something far, far, far. But now what I am telling you something as close as my mouth. One thing is clear. I have never seen where a lie overcomes truth. Take note of that. I have never seen where a lie overcomes truth. Truth will always prevail. I pray, Father, let your will be done. Let your will be done. Let your will be done. In Jesus' name.

It was a difficult message. The sense of unease was made the more acute by an incident that had occurred earlier at the church on Sunday, March 9, 2014. A young man who was affiliated with the terrorist group Boko Haram dramatically appeared in the church to confess of an attempt to bomb the church.[2] His name was Mustapha. He had travelled to Lagos in a group of five to bomb the church with a timed device.

The plan fell apart when they paused to eat at a restaurant across from the SCOAN. Emmanuel TV was broadcasting. A powerful broadcast prayer by T. B. Joshua supernaturally threw them into a state of confusion, and they fled from the scene, taking their bomb with them.

Four of the group members immediately departed from the area, but one of them found himself coming back to the church to confess. His name was Mustapha, a hardened militia-terrorist who was under strong occultic influence. But something profound had happened to him during that brief encounter with the televised prayer by T. B. Joshua.

"Anytime I lie down, I will be seeing you," he said to T. B. Joshua. He was exhausted and could not sleep. "You are disturbing me. I don't know what I did to you," he said.

When pressed further, he said he no longer had the desire to continue with his life of crime and murder. A second Boko Haram member was exposed and delivered in May of 2014. [3] His mission was to bomb churches. Both men were prayed for. Their cases were handed over to the authorities for investigation.

TRAGEDY STRIKES

On Friday, September 12, 2014, tragedy struck. The first sign of trouble was at 11:30 a.m. Observers were surprised to see a plane flying over the SCOAN guest house at a very low altitude. More disturbingly, the plane returned at 11:43 a.m., at 11:45 a.m., and finally at 11:54 a.m. The guest house imploded at 12:44 p.m. SCOAN security cameras captured the full sequence of events. [4] SCOAN visitors also captured images of the strange aircraft. [5] Among them were Shadrack Mamzini from South Africa. He recounted the event as follows:

> I wanted to take pictures of the Synagogue buildings. I took two pictures. While I was taking the last picture, I discovered a very big, giant aircraft. It was something which was unusual in the way it looked. It was not looking like a passenger flight or any ordinary flight. So, I asked myself what it was. I thought maybe it was because the airport was close, and the aircraft is going to land. My worry was that it was too low from the building.

Thobile Bhaku from South Africa also recounted the experience.

> I heard the aircraft, but I did not care about the aircraft. I went inside the dining hall because it was lunchtime. On the queue I was served. While I was preparing coffee for myself, I heard a big sound behind me. It was something like a big bang. When I looked up, I saw the slab falling down.

Mick Milambo from South Africa was walking with a friend when he saw the aircraft. "It was just passing here, slowly. A big aircraft. My friend told me, 'If you see an aircraft like this, it is trouble.'"

Charles Thawane from South African said, "The plane was big. It was moving very slowly. It did not look like an ordinary plane."

Prior to the incident, Prophet T. B. Joshua had placed surveillance cameras on the premises. One camera covered the front of the church, pointing upwards, showing the top of the building that collapsed. That is the direction from which the plane approached the building. He also had a second camera directed to the base of the building, pointing at the entrance area. The two cameras captured the full sequence of the flyby and the building collapse.[6] The camera pointing at the base of the building showed what looked like an explosion on the left side, facing the building. The building immediately crumpled into a pile of rubble and dust. This has to be one of the most documented building collapse.

THE AFTERMATH

There were loud calls for immediate action against the church, including calls for the immediate arrest of T. B. Joshua. As an example, Professors Olufemi Taiwo of Cornell University, Ebenezer Obadare of the University of Kansas, Akin Adesokan of Indiana University, Wale Adebanwi of the University of California, and Tejumola Olaniyan of the University of Wisconsin-Madison issued a widely cited joint statement calling for the arrest of T. B. Joshua.

They charged callousness, and neglect as the cause of the building collapse.[7] The statement which was issued in September came too early. There was nothing beyond various conflicting claims about what had happened. The hastiness and fury of the accusations was stunning.

As of 2020, there has yet to be presented incontrovertible evidence of fault on the part of the SCOAN. In fact, with time, the evidence has pointed the other way. A geotechnical expert and defense witness, Ebenezer Ologuntoye testified at the Lagos State High Court on March 21, 2019, that the foundation of the Synagogue of All Nations Church did not fail as has been alleged by the state.[8]

Ologuntoye's credentials are impeccable. He has consulted with a Polish company, Naeimor International, state governments in Nigeria, and Foundation Development Limited in London, among others. Samples from the site had been analyzed at the University of Lagos Laboratory and other laboratories using standard procedures.

Consensus reports were produced and signed off by representatives of the

SCOAN, the Lagos State Material Testing Laboratory and a Corona Court Representative.

"My findings on both reports show that the foundation did not fail, and the bearing capacity is adequate," Ologuntoye testified.

However, controversy has continued to swirl around the issue, with the former Nigerian Minister of Aviation Femi Fani-Kayode making pointed allegations that external forces carried out the act.

ODE TO MARTYRS

A total of one hundred and fifteen people died, with the majority being foreign visitors. The SCOAN has memorialized them as martyrs of faith. The professional opera singer, Kimmy Skota, sang a dirge for the deceased. Prophet T. B. Joshua composed the song. It opens with these words.

> Whether we die young or old, what matters is the grace to continue living hereafter. This world, people of God, is not our home. We are just passing through. We are living in the world, but we are not a part of it.

Skota's soprano voices rose, pregnant with questions. "Why? Why so soon? Heaven is our home. Why this time? Heaven is our reward. Why? Why this kind of death? Heaven knows. Heaven is our home. We long to be there. Heaven is our home."

The following condolence message was broadcast on Emmanuel TV

> We at Emmanuel TV and The Synagogue, Church of All Nations express our deepest condolences to the government of Nigeria, the government of South Africa and the governments of other affected nations, most especially the families, friends and loved ones of the precious souls who lost their lives in the tragic incident which occurred on Friday, September 12, 2014.

> May Almighty God console all and give courage and strength to bear the grievous losses. We pray that God's presence in our hearts and lives would more than supply their absence. Death to a believer is his release from the imprisonment of this world and his departure to the enjoyment of another world. Those who are born from

above long to be there. Those who lost their lives in the incident died not in vain but as martyrs of the Kingdom of God. As the Psalmist reflects, "Precious in the sight of the Lord is the death of His saints." (Ps 116:15 [NIV])

God's everlasting promise is to comfort all who mourn, provide for those who grieve, to bestow on them a crown of beauty for ashes, the oil of joy for mourning and a garment of praise for a spirit of despair. (Isa. 61:3 [NIV]) Trouble may endure for the night, but joy comes in the morning. To all, we greet you, good morning.

MY HOUR HAS NOT YET COME

T. B. Joshua is acquainted with loss. His father died when he was but a toddler. He lost his mother in the early years of his ministry. "What a wonderful woman!" he has said of her.

He has also lost beloved friends. But the 2014 loss was the most gut wrenching. Nevertheless, on the first Sunday after the building collapse, he was out praying for his guests. "My hour has not yet come," he said. "I have not yet finished my job."

Standing resolute and steadfast, in reverence of his God, and together with his disciples, he made it his finest hour. It was the way of the Master, the way of the cross. May it never happen again, we pray.

CHAPTER 10

A SERVANT IS NOT GREATER THAN HIS MASTER

The more things change, the more they remain the same," so goes a phrase coined by the French writer Jean-Baptiste Alphonse.

"Remember what I told you," our Lord said before his departure. "If they persecuted me, they will persecute you also. If they obeyed my teaching, they will obey yours also" (John 15:20 [NIV]).

The emergence of T. B. Joshua sent shock waves to a religious world that had grown complacent about the truth and power of the gospel message. The idea that the gospel could be preached with power and authority has scandalized the establishment. T. B. Joshua has taken comfort from the experiences of the early church.

"I look at the apostles in the Bible, the fire and temptations they went through. I see that history will tell us about my trials and temptation," T. B. Joshua said. "The most persecuted pastor. There is nothing I have not gone through in this country."

The early years of the SCOAN were make or break. Severe testing started in 1996 when T. B. Joshua was arrested on the false charge of drug dealing. An enemy had filed a false report. Persecution intensified as the ministry's outreach expanded, with a surge of international interest. Some who visited from Western countries sought the counsel of Nigerian pastors to help them make sense of this unexpected 'African' phenomenon. Among those who took an interest in T. B. Joshua's ministry were international pastors. They came away divided in their conclusions.

Among those who came away with a favorable conclusion were Canadian renewal leader John Arnott and New Zealand minister Bill Subritzky. Nevertheless, a well-documented campaign against T. B. Joshua also emerged. It was led by Nigerian pastors who actively campaigned against T. B. Joshua domestically and internationally. To this day, T. B. Joshua has been variously labelled as a practitioner of religious chicanery and an occultic figure, among other things.

Emmanuel TV, which was launched March 8, 2006, has been the primary instrument for contesting myths and disinformation about T. B. Joshua. Ironically, T. B. Joshua was forced to start Emmanuel TV when he was banned from broadcasting on Nigeria Television.

"Emmanuel TV came to rescue me," T. B. Joshua has said. "Now the story has become, 'Don't tell me. I watched live.'"

Even before 2006, there were indications that the Synagogue Church of All Nations was not going to be a passing fad. "Prominent Nigerian church leaders have labeled T.B. Joshua a fraud, but that has not stopped Christians in South Africa, Europe and the United States from continuing to support the controversial faith healer" wrote J. Lee Grady.

The power of T. B. Joshua's message has turned into a global tidal wave. As of 2020, visitors have come from across the globe, including Hong Kong, China, Vietnam, Egypt, Kazakhstan, Cambodia, Thailand, Japan, Russia, the Caribbean, Solomon Islands, India, Iran, Korea, Croatia, Ukraine, Pakistan, Brazil, Mexico, and the list goes on.

YouTube subscribers to Emmanuel TV exceeded 1.5 million in 2020. A YouTube video of T. B. Joshua's visit to an elderly community posted on January 26, 2020, attracted over half a million views in ten days (see picture). One prayer for viewers posted by the ministry had 3,455,134 views in January 2020. The song, "Sin's Power," composed by T. B. Joshua had garnered just under 1.2 million views at the end of January 2020.

I will now speak to specific controversies that have surrounded the work of T. B. Joshua. I have grouped them into four main themes. They are 1) his origins and mentorship; 2) that he is wealthy and self-enriching; 3) that the miracles are faked; and 4) that he uses evil powers. It is my contention that the fourth controversy has had the most negative impact.

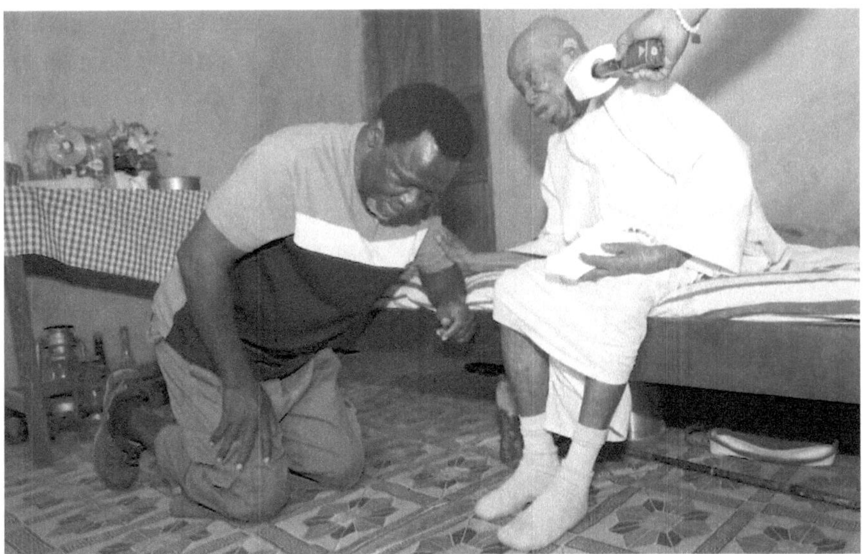

15. TB Joshua receives prayer from an elderly man

CONTROVERSY 1: T. B. JOSHUA HAS NO KNOWN MENTOR

When persons in the religious establishment have looked at T. B. Joshua, they have seen one unprepared and unfit to lead a globally acclaimed ministry. He has minimal education, is not a great orator, and he has no seminary training. But God chooses "the foolish things of the world to shame the wise." He chooses "the weak things of the world to shame the strong." (1 Cor. 1:27 [NIV]).

During one of his Sunday services, a pastor asked T. B. Joshua to pray for his admission to a university program to study for a master's degree. T. B. Joshua jokingly remarked that the person he was asking for prayer did not have a secondary school education. He then turned to him and asked a pointed question about his personal life. The episode spoke volumes about who T. B. Joshua is, his mission, and calling. There have been numerous other encounters between pastors and T. B. Joshua where he has revealed the greater things of the kingdom of God and helped them recover their true selves.

The Bible has many luminaries who emerged with no known mentor. They include John the Baptist, the Prophet Elijah, and the Prophet Amos who says of himself, "I was neither a prophet nor the son of a prophet, but I was a shepherd, and I also took care of sycamore-fig trees." (Amos 7:14 [NIV]).

In Acts chapter 4 we read the story of Peter and John before the Sanhedrin.

Before them was a previously lame man who had been restored. They had Peter and John brought before them and began to question them, "By what power or what name did you do this?"

Peter, filled with the Holy Spirit, famously responded:

> Rulers and elders of the people! If we are being called to account today for an act of kindness shown to a man who was lame and are being asked how he was healed, then know this, you and all the people of Israel: It is by the name of Jesus Christ of Nazareth, whom you crucified but whom God raised from the dead, that this man stands before you healed. (Acts 4:8-10 [NIV])

When the men of the Sanhedrin saw the courage of Peter and John and realized that they were unschooled, ordinary men, they were astonished, and they took note that these men had been with Jesus. During his earthly ministry Jesus also surprised the Jewish spiritual leadership. They were "astonished," and remarked, "How can this man be so educated when he has never gone to school?" (John 7:15 [NIV]).

Jesus's humble background was also a barrier for those who had known him growing up. This is what they said of him when he returned to his hometown.

> Where did this man get this wisdom and these miraculous powers? Isn't this the carpenter's son? Isn't his mother's name Mary, and aren't his brothers James, Joseph, Simon and Judas? Aren't all his sisters with us? Where then did this man get all these things? And they took offence at him. (Matt. 13: 54-57 [NIV])

Based on how God has acted in the past, it is abundantly clear that the criticism about T. B. Joshua's formal training is unbiblical and completely without merit. God acts as He wills. "Who has known the mind of the Lord? Or who has been his counselor?" (Rom. 11:34 [NIV]).

As the apostle Paul has said, "The person without the Spirit does not accept the things that come from the Spirit of God but considers them foolishness and cannot understand them because they are discerned only through the Spirit." (1 Cor. 2:14 [NIV])

T. B. Joshua has spoken very clearly about these matters, emphasizing the vital importance of depending on God alone. Here are his words.

We Christians depend on God's Spirit for strength and assistance. That makes us Christians different from religious people. Christians depend on God's Spirit to worship. The mind is renewed by studying the Word and acting on it. It is not only committing the Word to memory, which is valuable, but it is letting the Word become an integral part of your being. The Word builds Christ's nature. God is building himself into us, making himself a part of us by dominating, ruling, and sanctifying our spirit nature. You cannot build one up spiritually on philosophies or theory of the Word or on the history of the Word. We are made spiritual by living in the Word and by the Word living in us.

Are you depending on God's Spirit to teach people? If you are not depending on God's Word to teach people, you are only teaching them history. If you are not dependent on God's Spirit to preach this message and you just take it because you are educated, you pick it because you have the speaking skills, you are teaching them history and literature. God's Word is Spirit. As Christians we depend on God's Spirit to worship. If you are not dependent on God's Spirit to teach, to preach, to worship, you are a religious man.

CONTROVERSY 2: T. B. JOSHUA IS A SELF-ENRICHING PASTOR OF A MEGACHURCH

A second line of criticism of T. B. Joshua is that he is a self-enriching pastor.[1] This criticism has gained the least traction in public perceptions of T. B. Joshua, based on my review of social media commentary. The overwhelming nature of T. B. Joshua's charity work, and his simple personal lifestyle are the primary reason. He has stood out in his compelling teachings about the corroding power of money in the church.[2] Even then, *Forbes* magazine published an article entitled "Five Richest Pastors in Nigeria." T. B. Joshua's personal wealth was estimated at $10-15 million.

The idea that T. B. Joshua's ministry is motivated by personal gain and monetary reward is easy to dispel. A few examples will suffice. On June 1, 2019, T. B. Joshua ministries staged a large event in Sheffield, England, at the FlyDSA arena. The arena sits 13,000, but the attendance was much higher since there were thousands sitting on the floor of the arena. Attendance was free. No offering was taken. Attendees were asked to go back to their communities and help people in need. "You have received so much. It is time for you to give back," they were told.[3]

T. B. Joshua has a policy of not taking a collection at international crusades. He does not organize an event for which he cannot pay. He has repeatedly warned congregants and pastors of the corrupting power of money. "The weakness of everyone here is pride," he said during one service. "We need to humble ourselves. We are too proud. That is why we believe so much in money. Wherever money asks you to go you will go. When you speak, one can hear the voice of money."

In a 2019 message, T. B. Joshua spoke of having received a revelation from God warning him to not focus on growth and numbers. He surprised everyone when he immediately reduced the seating capacity of the church auditorium. He also closed the overflow section. In 2018 he had presented a message where he said, "Don't let money control you. Let the Giver of that money control you." The following is the essence of what he said then.[4]

> We are not here because of the offering. We are here because of the souls. Some of us are coming from a very small church. It's good! It's not the size of the ministry that determines the strength of the ministry. The strength of the ministry is not in its large population, branches all over, or being the biggest church in the world. It is not the number of people that enter here that matters, but the souls that are being saved. I learned this from apostles of old. How many of them had what we call a church? They evangelized all over. We are looking for crowds today. But what of the soul?

On January 13, 2020, Prophet T. B. Joshua spoke again on the matter of offerings. The occasion was a special healing service.[5]

> Whom should we be asking for support? Distressed people? The sick? Worried people? We cannot begin bothering distressed people, the sick ones, and the poor ones by asking for financial support, though it is scriptural. When you are distressed, your "thank you" is distressed. When you are sick, your "thank you" is sick.
>
> You cannot live above your word. What you are going to say, you must mean it. Your heart will tell you whom you are. It's a thing of

the heart. Many people borrow money to be here. Are we asking them to give out of the money they borrowed for offering? Appearance is deceptive. That is why most gifts today are a curse, not a blessing. Most offerings collected in churches all over the world today are a curse, not a blessing.

This is not to say the SCOAN does not encourage giving. The heart of the issue is that offering should be freely given. "The point is this: whoever sows sparingly will also reap sparingly, and whoever sows bountifully will also reap bountifully. Each one must give as he has decided in his heart, not reluctantly or under compulsion, for God loves a cheerful giver." (2 Cor. 9:6-7 [NIV])

T. B. Joshua told the congregation they would be more freely able to give later. "When you are delivered, your 'thank you' is a blessing from God," he said.

CONTROVERSY 3:
THE MIRACLES ARE FAKED

Stories emerging from the popular press and secular writers have sought to portray claims of healing as not only fake, but as a danger to public health. The reporting has been based on hearsay. One gets the clear impression that the subject of healing is not considered worthy of serious investigation. A case in point is the October 2011 story by Andy Dangerfield of BBC News. The BBC reported unconfirmed HIV/ADS related deaths in London. [6] It was further alleged that the deceased had stopped taking medication following prayers at a church in London. The church was not named. The Synagogue Church of All Nations, which then had a branch in London, was cited as one of the places where people were encouraged "to abandon HIV drug treatments in favor of prayer."

The story devoted close to forty percent of the text to the SCOAN. Two large photographs taken from the SCOAN website were also included. The effect was to create a strong climate of opinion that the SCOAN bore responsibility for the alleged deaths. Some of the more discerning online comments noted that the "the three [alleged deaths] in question have no demonstrable link to the SCOAN." [7]

The BBC story immediately had legs. Sky News (UK) quickly followed up by dispatching an undercover team to the London branch of the SCOAN with hidden cameras. The report was sensational but inconclusive. The storyline was picked up by the Christian Post, and the New York based Sahara News, among other news outlets. "Church Claiming It Can 'Pray the AIDS Away' Blamed for 6 Premature Deaths," declared Ray Downs of the Christian Post.[8]

The number of deaths had suddenly doubled. "Millionaire Nigerian Pastor T. B. Joshua's Church Linked to Fraudulent AIDS Claims," blared the headline from Sahara Reporters.[9]

Sloane Speakman of Vanderbilt University cited the BBC story in a paper entitled "Comparing the Impact of Religious Discourse on HIV/AIDS in Islam and Christianity in Africa."[10]

The article said in part, "Under the leadership of T.B. Joshua, Nigeria's third richest clergyman, the church has come under criticism in recent months for advising their congregations to stop taking lifesaving HIV medication."

This work has, in turn, been cited by others. The mythical connection between the alleged deaths and T. B. Joshua was firmly planted.

Among those citing the BBC story was Rowan Moore Gerety. He wrote a critical story on T. B. Joshua's ministry that appeared in *Foreign Policy* on April 25, 2014.[11] His work was supported by a grant from the International Reporting Project (IRP) whose mission was to fund "independent journalistic coverage of under-reported events around the world."[12]

Gerety was primarily concerned with voicing the concern that sick people "were interrupting or deferring orthodox treatment altogether in favor of the divine," and that healing ministries, especially T. B. Joshua's church were responsible.

According to his reporting, "the BBC named T.B. Joshua in an investigation into the deaths of three HIV-positive African women living in London." This is of course not true. The deaths were only alleged, and there was no investigation launched on T. B. Joshua. He also wrote that T.B. Joshua was controversial "even among fellow faith leaders," which was true with regard to the Pentecostal Fellowship of Nigeria (PFN).

I discuss this later in this chapter. The overall effect of the story has always been to reinforce an image of T. B. Joshua as pretentious and the ministry as a societal problem.

Gerety's primary concern was that "patients were interrupting or deferring orthodox treatment altogether in favor of the divine." It is difficult to appreciate the merit of the claim for two reasons. First, Nigeria's population is in excess of two hundred million, of which the proportion that has visited the SCOAN is insignificant.

The second and more compelling point is that there is nothing in Gerety's report that contests the central claim of the SCOAN that God heals. Quite on the contrary, the unfolding evidence of healing was literally staring him in the face during his 2013 visit to the SCOAN, but he was perhaps in too much of a hurry to document it. One need go no further than the photograph of the bleeding woman that he shot and featured in his story.

The woman is unnamed in the story, which is a telltale sign. She is, in fact, Mrs. Rosemary Imma whom I presented in chapter 7. This case has been thoroughly confirmed. Gerety struggled to make sense of the healing session at the SCOAN. "[E]ventually, it became overwhelming, and I walked out into the street," he has written.

A systematic inquiry was called for. As I noted earlier, Mrs. Imma appeared at the church two more times, a week later to celebrate the healing, and some months later to thank God for her life and the birth of her baby. Regrettably, the snapshot type inquiry of the Foreign Policy report is characteristic of most reports that have appeared in the media.

The veracity of the miracles at the SCOAN has in fact been confirmed by many people. Writing in 2002, Tjerk W. Muller a prominent Dutch critic of T. B. Joshua has said as much. "The miraculous events that take place around the person of T. B. Joshua are now well known," he wrote.

He was writing at a time when over "a thousand Dutch people" were reported to have travelled to Lagos "to receive healing there or to see God's salvation."

Muller himself did not travel to Lagos. One who did was Willem J. Ouweneel, a leading philosopher and theologian. He was persuaded to visit by his daughter, Josien Baksteen. She and her husband Hans had visited the Synagogue Church of All Nations in March of 2002, to be prayed for because they could not have a baby. After Prophet T.B. Joshua prayed for the couple, Josie Baksteen conceived, and the couple had a baby girl. Following his visit, Ouweneel received healing from an ailment.

It is reported that when people have questioned the veracity of the miracles at the SCOAN, he has simply pointed to his granddaughter as proof. "Look here, she is the miracle," he has said"[13]

Independent confirmations of healings have also come from the American, Jerrell Miller, editor of *The Remnant International*. In 2003 and 2004, Miller travelled to Lagos, spending some twenty-one days at the church. "My friends, the healings are real in Africa, lives are being touched and the full glory has not yet been revealed," he reported.[14]

According to J. Lee Grady, former editor of the Christian magazine *Charisma,* "Joshua's critics, including prominent pastors in the country, won't deny that he heals people. But they say he draws his power from indigenous African occultism—not from the Holy Spirit."[15]

In summary, the evidence of healings on a massive scale at the SCOAN has not been seriously disputed by either friends or foe. Those who have questioned these stories have yet to prove that they invested time to systematically review the evidence.

By the time Gerety arrived at the SCOAN in 2013, the debate had long shifted from whether miracles occur, to the question of how they were possible. This question has generated its own controversies and warrants a more extended discussion. The controversy has centered on the claim that T. B. Joshua uses evil powers.

CONTROVERSY 4:
T. B. JOSHUA USES EVIL POWERS

The Epicenter of the Controversy

In July 2002, members of the Pentecostal Fellowship of Nigeria (PFN) held a critical meeting in Lagos and T. B. Joshua was on the agenda. The meeting has been recognized as a critical event in the broken relation between T. B. Joshua and Nigerian pastors.[16] Allegations were made that he "mixes Christianity with occult practices."[17]

Among those present was a "group of Americans that included theologian C. Peter Wagner, Colorado pastor Ted Haggard, and prayer leader Chuck Pierce."[18] The message to the foreign pastors was that T.B. Joshua was "dangerous to the body of Christ, both in Nigeria and globally." The healings were not to be taken at face value. The visitors needed to understand that "witchdoctors have healed many people" in Nigeria.[19]

It is reported that "the pastors joined hands and prayed that God would prevent Joshua from deceiving Christians with false miracles."[20]

The views of foreign pastors opposed to T. B. Joshua, then and now, have been shaped by the forceful opposition from their Nigerian counterparts. "Our brothers in Nigeria are on the ground there, and they know best," one prominent foreign leader is reported to have said.[21]

The T. B. Joshua controversy had been brewing up for some time before the 2002 meeting. Towards the end of 2001, reports emerged that Pastor Chris Oyakhilome, had visited T. B. Joshua.[22] The totality of the PFN membership was outraged and threatened to cut off links with any Pentecostal pastor "who fraternizes" with him.[23]

The press also played a part in disseminating myths and false allegations about "occultic practices" at the SCOAN.[24] Matters came to a head when the PFN instigated an outright ban on the broadcasting of miracle services.[25] The banning order was issued on March 30, 2004, by the National Broadcasting Commission (NBC).[26] Although no persons were named, T. B. Joshua was the primary target.[27]

The allegations against T. B. Joshua were challenged by a core of international evangelical pastors. These pastors had taken time to visit T. B. Joshua, which set them apart from the opposing group. Among them were the "Canadian John Arnott, Pittsburgh pastor Joseph Garlington, Louisiana evangelist Marvin Gorman, and New Zealand minister Bill Subritzky."[28]

Jerrell Miller, editor of American publication, *The Remnant International* also became a strong supporter of T. B. Joshua. Over several visits, he spent a total of twenty-one days at the SCOAN.

The Dutch philosopher and theologian, Willem J. Ouweneel, also endorsed T. B. Joshua following the miracle of his granddaughter's birth. He made several personal visits to the SCOAN.

J. Lee Grady from the United States emerged as a leading voice against T. B. Joshua within the United States and internationally. He visited Nigeria in 2002. He was at that time editor of *Charisma,* a position he held for eleven years. *Charisma* has been a leading Christian magazine that represents Pentecostal and charismatic Christians in the United States. In 2005, *TIME* magazine named *Charisma*'s founder Steve Strang one of "The Most Influential Evangelicals in America." Lee Grady spent some time meeting with Nigerian pastors opposed to T. B. Joshua, and later visited the SCOAN.

Following his visit to Nigeria, he published reports on T. B. Joshua. "Some Nigerian leaders claim animal sacrifices have been performed in Joshua's church to generate a source for occult power," he reported.[29] According to him, "Pentecostal leaders had denounced him publicly because of his occult background and because he mixed Christian terminology with pagan healing methods."[30]

He also reported allegations of illicit sexual practices.[31] Although Lee Grady was afforded an audience with T. B. Joshua, he was pre-occupied with seeking confirmation of what he had been told. He wrote:

I finally sat down with Joshua. After being in his offices, talking with his zombie-like followers, interviewing ex-members of his cult and watching videos of his bizarre methods (which include a form of magic writing), my own gut feelings confirmed what I had already been told by countless pastors in Lagos, Port Harcourt, Abuja and other cities: This man was not operating by the Holy Spirit's power.[32]

It is quite preposterous to characterize T. B. Joshua's team of evangelists as zombie-like. One is hard-pressed to find anywhere in the church today where a pastor has groomed young men and women of such a high caliber. We have seen them preaching, healing, delivering and manifesting the gifts of prophecy with T. B. Joshua in the background. That is the hallmark of a great teacher.

Jerrell Miller, editor of *The Remnant International,* happened to be at the Synagogue Church of All Nations when Lee Grady visited for his interview with T. B. Joshua. He was stunned and shocked by his report. "Many horror stories are being written about Joshua, but this time those who are writing have gone all the way to the gutter," he reported. Miller revealed that Lee Grady had "spent just one-half hour" with T. B. Joshua. In contrast, he had spent twenty-one days at the church.

"I have learned one thing about this man," he reported. "He is kind, loving toward his family, and dedicated to the Gospel of Jesus Christ. I watched how he works with his people, and he is nothing like what was written about him. One thing Joshua knows about his calling is that it comes complete with critics. He also knows that when critics begin to tear, the glory begins to come in."

The Controversy Spills over into The Netherlands

On April 20, 2002, Hanke Helms from the Netherlands wrote a news article about T. B. Joshua, in the *Nederllands Dagblad,* a Dutch daily newspaper.[33] He was particularly interested in the case of a Mr. Jan Westerhof from Doetinchem who had gone to the SCOAN wheelchair bound as he suffered from multiple sclerosis. To everyone's surprise, he returned healed.

An archival video of the Jan Westerhof healing may be viewed using the link provided.[34]

Stories about T. B. Joshua appeared in *Visie van de EO,* the largest Christian magazine in the Netherlands, the evangelical monthly newspaper *Challenge,* and the charismatic news service *Joel News.* The coverage was quite mixed. As

Helms has reported, Westerhof's story "caused much turmoil within the Baptist church in Doetinchem." This was Westerhof's church.

While the healing was self-evident, it had raised "questions within the congregation about the source from which T. B. Joshua heals people. Is that occult?"

There was even fear that Westerhof might carry an evil spirit as a result of his encounter with T. B. Joshua. "If Westerhof were infected by a wrong spirit, would that spirit not be able to penetrate the church through him?"

It should be noted that the Dutch were familiar with Lee Grady's critical report on T. B. Joshua.

Following the reports of miracles, Bert Panhuise, chairman of EuroSpirit and Arie Potuyt of Messiah Television Rotterdam travelled to the SCOAN. Their mission was to make television recordings for T. B. N. Europe. "What they experienced there raised so many questions with them that they decided not to broadcast the film material for the time being," *Joel News* reported. [35]

It is not clear what Bert Panhuise and Arie Potuyt found so troubling. The reports that followed pointed to doctrinal questions about water baptism, the Holy Communion, and speaking in tongues. [36] Other points of contention were about how T. B. Joshua could "manipulate people from a distance with hand movements," and miscellaneous observations such as these. [37] T. B. Joshua has at various points spoken about such controversies in the church. Here is some of what he has said.

> As Christians, we depend on God's Spirit to worship. If you are not depending on God's Spirit, you are a religious man. When I say religious, I mean they live by senses. They live by what they see. When you live by what you see, no matter the knowledge of the Bible you have, you are a religious man. If we depend on God's Spirit to worship, there is no controversy

A video clip of the Dutch visitors at the SCOAN surfaced in 2020. They are shown interviewing T. B. Joshua. The video does not give any hint of a controversy. Indeed, the visitors are shown heaping praises on T. B. Joshua on camera. T. B. Joshua appeared taken aback. With characteristic humility he said,

> This is a wonderful message. T. B. Joshua should not allow this message to go into his head. T. B. Joshua should just have to seek more of His grace. The goodness and kindness. He can still do more,

better than this. So, he should keep pressing. You too can do even better than T. B. Joshua, if only you mirror Him all the time, not occasionally.[38]

T. B. Joshua also said this to the Dutch group,

> The Bible says the Holy Spirit opens our eyes to see what is promised to us in Christ Jesus. Without the Holy Spirit, we cannot see what is promised to us. You only hear miracles, but you never see miracles. You only hear salvation; you only hear preaching and teaching in the power of the Holy Ghost. But with the power of the Holy Ghost, you see what is promised to us—salvation is promised to us, miracle is promised to us, and all of God's blessings. But Holy Spirit is the supplier. So, if you know Jesus, you must know Holy Spirit.

The controversy boiled down to how to reconcile two conflicting positions. On one hand, there was indisputable evidence of miracles on a massive scale. Yet on the other hand, the experts could not bring themselves to believe T. B. Joshua was Christian. "As of 2002, the Evangelical Netherlands is concerned with whether T. B. Joshua, a successful preacher from Lagos, Nigeria, is bona fide," wrote Tjerk W. Muller.[39]

To reconcile the contradictions, the idea that T. B. Joshua's ministry was a manifestation of a mixed kingdom took hold among some influential circles. I discuss that next.

The Mixed Kingdom Controversy

The mixed kingdom resolution is the claim that T. B. Joshua "mixes Christianity with occult practices." There are indications that the term had origins within Nigeria, and the Dutch scholars merely appropriated it.[40] Lee Grady says as much. He wrote, "The Pentecostal leaders had denounced him publicly because of his occult background and because he mixed Christian terminology with pagan healing methods."

Within The Netherlands, the term was brought forward in a report by the *Joel News*. "There are powerful healings in the Synagogue, for which God has the honor," the publication reported. "And there is sectarianism and demonic influence," the report added.

The term immediately provoked sharp criticism from the evangelical monthly magazine, *Uitdaging*. Tjerk W. Muller's 2002 article entitled "How Do People Assess the T. B. Joshua Phenomenon?" provides some insight into these debates. Any objective observer would have no reason to doubt that "beautiful things are taking place in Lagos, Nigeria in the Name of the Lord God and Jesus Christ," he wrote at the same time, he charged that there were "animistic-looking elements in Joshua's practice" stemming from his African background. He would therefore not recommend visits to Lagos even for cases where there was little or no hope of a cure through medicine. Muller then went into an extended and apparently learned discussion of the parallels between what was happening in Lagos and pagan Canaanite cultures in the Old Testament as well as Eastern paganism. The argument is quite opaque and difficult to make sense of.[41]

Does God Not Work in the Netherlands?

Of greater concern to Muller and others was why the phenomena observed in Lagos were not also observed in the Netherlands, if they were truly from God. "God is a universal God, a God who cannot be located in one place, but omnipresent."

The presence of miracles in Lagos therefore raised serious questions. "If God does not heal someone in the Netherlands … why should he heal that person in Nigeria? Is God bound by places or persons?"

The Netherlands had many committed Christians. They also had people who believed that God "wants to work miracles and healings even today."

Indeed, the Netherlands, and more broadly Europe had an established history in the Christian faith. It was therefore fitting that these greater works of God should occur there rather than Nigeria, if they were to occur at all. "It is precisely in the Netherlands that the apostolic message is preserved, and baptism and sacrament are celebrated, as our Lord has instructed his disciples. Is there now nobody in the Netherlands, or in that respect Germany, Belgium, France or Great Britain by whom God would like to work? Is the Holy Spirit really more present in Lagos Nigeria than in Leiderdorp or Aalsmeer, the Netherlands?"[42]

The negative aspersions on Nigeria from Muller were unrelenting. "I do not believe that the Netherlands would be more corrupt than Nigeria. It is not for nothing that Nigeria is a country that has the largest numbers of HIV infections worldwide."

African existence was "still dominated by shamans and naturopaths, superstitions and ancient rites that control life and death. Corruption, wars, and dictatorial regimes also flourish." Muller concludes, "In short, I don't see why the spiritual climate in the Netherlands, or the West, would prevent the Lord God from doing more wonderful things than in any other continent or country in the world. And if God does not heal or deliver someone in the Netherlands, I cannot see why He would suddenly do it in Nigeria."

These arguments may seem to make sense in the natural, but the Word of God is not of human or natural origins. It has always been preceded by revelation. He acts as He wills. He looks at the heart. He chose David over his brothers. He chose Mary of Nazareth over everyone else. "My soul glorifies the Lord and my spirit rejoices in God my Savior, for he has been mindful of the humble state of his servant," Mary proclaimed.

The mystery of T. B. Joshua is the mystery of God.

The debates about T. B. Joshua created significant stress within the church in The Netherlands. In 2005, Gerard ter Horst, editor of *Nederlands Dagblad*, penned an assessment of the situation. Divisions about T. B. Joshua had persisted, he reported, but the active confrontations were no more. "Both camps acknowledge that discussions are silent, and say they cherish the peace."

Others, such as Willem Ouweneel continued to express "respect and admiration" for T. B. Joshua. "If God is going to do his work, it often causes unrest," Ouweneel is reported to have said.

T. B. JOSHUA, DESTINED
TO BE SPOKEN AGAINST

The depth and intensity of attacks on T. B. Joshua intensified, spreading to other countries. "I was shocked by what I found about Joshua on the internet", Professor Ouweneel is reported to have said.

Nothing seemed to be off bounds as some of the most virulent critics threw the kitchen sink at him. Even the theologian Tjerk W. Muller, who came out strongly against T. B. Joshua agreed with Ouweneel that "some criticism such as that found on the internet is purely intended to find something against Joshua."

Many fringe sources claiming a Christian mantle attacked T. B. Joshua with nothing but hearsay. *Charisma*, which was considered mainstream, was a surprise letdown. The people at *Charisma* had "become very raw in their stories" about T. B. Joshua, and "the very credibility of this magazine in the body of

Christ to tell the truth has caused many to question their methods," wrote Jerrell Miller, editor of *The Remnant International.*

The reality is that the attacks on T. B. Joshua never abated, but in the early days when his work was less known, the force of the falsehoods would have derailed someone without a clear sense of calling.

THE VALUE OF HIS TRIALS

KNOWING GOD'S OPINION

In this chapter I present words of wisdom from Prophet T. B. Joshua.[1] They help to us to understand how he has managed the burdens of his ministry, the persecution, name calling, and other challenges. He wants his hearers to understand that "Life does not just happen to us. It is all about choices and how we respond to every situation."

He also wants people to understand that "accepting Jesus as your Lord and Savior does not mean trial will not come."

There will be good and hard times alike, but when "we know God's opinion about all situations, it settles all things." Knowing God's opinion imparts strength to the believer to endure and creates the right conditions for God's rescue.

THE VALUE OF TESTING

On the value of testing, T. B. Joshua has shared the following counsel.

Personal improvement and fulfillment come through the continual process of learning from both negative and positive experiences. When times are stable and the seas are calm and secure, no one is really tested. People will challenge you, question you, try to get you off track; don't listen to the temptation to act out of character. Be strong in challenges, believing that your personal achievement, your personal improvement, and fulfillment come through the continual process of learning from both negative and positive experiences.

When we have exhausted our mental and emotional resources, we can no longer rely on ourselves. You simply have to trust on something, on someone stronger, wiser, and smarter than yourself.

Jesus, who raised the dead, was Paul's choice.[2] What is yours? He delivered Paul from hardship, burden, trouble, and death. They learned not to rely on themselves, but on God Almighty. He has rescued you in the past. He will rescue you now, and He will in the future.

In every situation, God has something to say. Even when He seems to be quiet, He is still saying something. I want to tell you one of the blessings God gave to me. I feel strong in challenges believing that personal improvement and fulfillment come through the continual process of learning from both positive and negative experiences.

You persecute me, you call me names. Whatever you call me, it's a blessing to me. Personal improvement and fulfillment come through the continual process of learning from both negative and positive experiences. "He is this, he is that." This makes me strong today. There is a school of persecution, a school of intimidation, a school of praises, and breakthrough. You must attend. You must have degrees in both universities.

A LESSON FROM HIS MOTHER

If you are a Christian, crises and situations are friends and not your enemy. When you begin to see your situation as a friend, you will overcome it. Situations are meant to promote you. They are meant for your spiritual growth. When you accept Jesus as your Lord and Saviour and renounce your past and follow Him, whatever situation you are facing is for your spiritual benefit.

The day you accept Jesus as your Lord and Saviour with all your heart, and you mean it, whatever situation you are facing is for your spiritual benefit. Let me pay tribute to my late mother. She used to say when times are stable and the seas are calm and secure, no one is really tested.

TRUE CHRISTIANS DON'T ALLOW THEIR SITUATIONS TO RULE THEM

A life motivated by love will not be controlled by situations but will master them. This was the essence of T. B. Joshua's message when he cited John 16:33. "I have told you these things so that in me you may have peace. In this world you will have trouble."

He warned that Satan wants believers to lament, complain, and curse God. He wants to separate them from their Creator and overthrow them from their position. "But those who bless God in their trouble prove their sonship."

The Bible teaches that when we face challenges, we should call on Him. "He has promised to honor those who honor him. He promised to bless those who bless Him when certain things seem not alright."

We are not to wait till trouble is over to bless the name of the Lord.

> When we commit a certain matter to our Lord Jesus Christ, our attitude towards that matter should change greatly. It should prove that really, we committed the matter to God.
>
> Who told you that when you become a Christian you would not face challenges? Where did you read it in the Bible that when you become a Christian, you will not fall sick? Where did you read it that when you become a Christian, your business will not go up, down, up, down? When you become a Christian, something will not touch you, hit you? Who told you this?
>
> This is why Jesus said to you, "I pray your faith will not fail." If there would not be challenges, Jesus would not say that. "I pray your faith will not fail"
>
> It means there will be something that will test your faith, your movement with Him, and your journey with Him. Something will try to stop you; something will try to discourage you. Because you believe that once you become a Christian there will be no sickness, no trouble, no attack, you allow your situation to rule you. Your situation will tell you whether you are a Christian or not. True Christian don't allow their situations to rule them, because they know that in our walking with the Lord, there are good and hard times.[3]

A KEY THAT WILL HELP YOUR LIFE

I want to give you a key that will help your life. Any time you are facing a situation or a challenge, it is time to honor Jesus before men. When situations come, Satan wants you to be sad. That sadness is not permitted by the Holy Spirit because the Holy Spirit wants a free spirit to operate. Your spirit must be free and if your spirit is free, joy and happiness come.

But when your spirit is not free and you are worried, the Holy Spirit is not allowed to work at that moment. So Satan wants you to be sad. To be sad is to be out of God. He doesn't want you to be with God but wants you to be out of God.

When you are not happy, you cannot make any good decision. It means you cannot pray and if you try to pray you are praying to yourself. People around you will hear you, but God will not hear you. Can you see the need to be happy and joyful even when there is nothing to be happy about?

What Satan wants to achieve is to take you out of God. The moment you are not happy, you are out of God. Satan can attack you. He can have access to you. I am not saying create happiness. I am talking about a natural happiness that comes as a result of your deeds. When a situation comes, you can still hold onto your joy. Quickly remember what the Bible says, "In this world amidst that tribulation, cheer up!"

God wants to have access to you while you are in trouble, and to have access to you, you have to be happy in that trouble so that He can come and rescue you. These are the decisions we have to make when we follow Him. If you mean it with all your heart, the more that attack, the more your desire for God. But when you don't mean it, and the attack comes, you will look back and begin to see Jesus in a bad light.

Paul said in the book of Romans, "What can separate me from the love of God?" Because he meant it, he said it with all his heart. Indeed, trouble and tribulation came; there was nothing that did not come to Paul. But the more those things came, the more was his desire for God.

What is holy we attack and what is dirty we don't attack. If you are not worth it, no-one will attack you. The attack on you shows your potential value. If you are worth it, you deserve attack from those who are not worth it. You can never envy someone who is below you but someone above you. You have decided to follow Jesus. Mean it. Someone is coming to ask you. Someone is coming to confirm. Mean it.

These words are more than sufficient to explain how and why T. B. Joshua has continued to prosper in the face of fierce opposition. There is much to reflect on from this experience.

CHAPTER 12

A NEW FORM OF CHRISTIANITY

want to finish this book by turning back to the words in chapter 2. There I highlighted T. B. Joshua's foundational belief, which is this, "Ministry does not begin with a relationship with people. It begins with a relationship with God. That relationship overflows to people."

He then says this. "The kind of relationship that I am talking about has to do with love." His life has been a living laboratory of a total commitment to this teaching. The scripture that best captures the teaching is well known. It is Matthew 22: 37-40.

> One of them, an expert in the law, tested him with this question: "Teacher, which is the greatest commandment in the Law?" Jesus replied, "Love the Lord your God with all your heart and with all your soul and with all your mind." This is the first and greatest commandment. And the second is like it: "Love your neighbor as yourself." All the Law and the Prophets hang on these two commandments.

We learn from these words that love is an integral part of the office of Prophet. This is clear when the Lord Jesus says, "All the Law *and the Prophets* hang on these two commandments."

The principle of love is thus the mystery of T. B. Joshua, who has been a prophet of God. When you understand this, you are no longer baffled by his actions, how he relates to the world, and to friend and foe. But this does not stop there. The message is for all followers of Christ.

As T. B. Joshua teaches, "As a Christian you are not a common man. You are a supernatural man. A common man is someone who does not know where he is going, and where he is coming from."

For those who are truly born again in Christ, there is a natural outflow of "love without expectation."

What does T. B. Joshua mean by this? *"When we love without expectation, our love is being sown to the Spirit. Anything you do to carry God along; you are doing it in Spirit because God is Spirit—I mean, total humility and submission to His will."*[1]

As Apostle Paul has put it, "I have been crucified with Christ and I no longer live, but Christ lives in me. The life I now live in the body, I live by faith in the Son of God, who loved me and gave himself for me." (Gal. 2:20 [NIV])

LOVE SEEKS TO TURN ENEMIES INTO FRIENDS

A life motivated by love does not judge others and always seeks to build broken relationships for the greater good, even turning enemies into friends. While the attacks on him have been well documented, T. B. Joshua has always been forward looking, seeking to build, and looking beyond himself.

> Sometimes, you will see me very quiet. With all that you are saying about me for the past thirty years, that "I am this; I am that" I will not talk. This is the reason—I am being very careful. You can abuse me, say all sorts of things against me, but I will not talk. I will give myself to prayer. Someone who is a devil to you, pain to you today, may be the savior tomorrow. You can be whatever you are to me today. If you are a devil to me today, I will look beyond you to see what you may become tomorrow. Tomorrow is a mystery. In relationships—be careful. The person who is your enemy today can be your savior tomorrow. If you continue to use the actions of people today to judge them, you may have problems in the future.[2]

This was demonstrated when Pastor Gabriel Ikpenwa came to the SCOAN with his wife and baby child.[3] He had a confession to make. "I have preached a lot of messages against the man of God [T. B. Joshua] as the antichrist of our generation," he tearfully spoke.

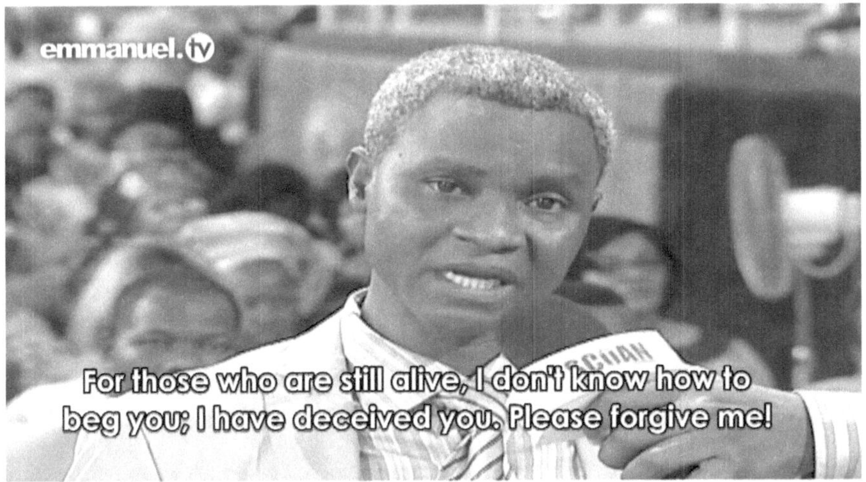

16. Pastor Gabriel Ikpenwa at the SCOAN

This was based on falsehoods he had accepted from other pastors who were his seniors. He came to T. B. Joshua as a last resort and in great distress, facing a storm of marital and financial troubles. He had exhausted all the sources of help that he trusted, nationally and from outside the country.

He found himself drawn to the 'evil' channel, Emmanuel TV, but he would not let anyone catch him watching it. The secret watching turned to genuine interest as long-held myths were dispelled. He came to the uncomfortable realization that the man he had so ferociously opposed might be the instrument for his release.

He decided to visit the SCOAN. Two secret visits followed. He came in disguise. The third visit was with his wife and this time he sought prayers. The demonic powers that had strangled their lives were exposed and cast out. Pastor Gabriel Ikpenwa was overwhelmed with both gratitude and regret. He wept publicly, grieving over the many people he had led astray.

> Please man of God, I don't know how to say it. I beg that you forgive me. Why I am saying this is because I know many people may have received deliverance as I have received, but because of my talk, many people who should have received deliverance did not because

I told them not to come here. Through my ministry many have been saved, but coming to this ministry, I have fought it with all my vein as a youth. I have fought it with all my muscle that nobody should come here.

T. B. Joshua responded with kindness and grace. He counseled that every genuine leader should take time to confirm what they hear. He also said that the matters they were talking about were of the Spirit. They were not there to debate. "You have seen the reward in my life. If not the condemnation and the persecution, do you think I would be at this level that I am today? I know the value of my trials. The value is so great. It made the whole world to know me."

YOU HIDE UNDER THE BIBLE. AND YOU KEEP SAYING JESUS

T. B. Joshua has warned those who claim to be Christians to carefully examine themselves in the light of God's standard, and specifically on love. The apostle Paul has said the same thing with these words, "Do not think of yourself more highly than you ought, but rather think of yourself with sober judgment, in accordance with the measure of faith God has given you." (Rom. 12:3 [NIV])

In a challenge to professing Christians, he has cited the example of former President Umaru Musa Yar'Adua who was a Muslim. He has recounted how the president bestowed a national honor on him while others who profess the Christian faith have vilified him. The president personally called T. B. Joshua to say he needed to be honored.

This is a man that does not share the same faith with me. He is a Muslim man. Why I am saying this is that sometimes, you talk of North, you talk of South, you talk of Christian, religion or whatever. You forget love. Where is love? Love is the greatest. The Bible says love your neighbor as yourself. Your neighbor could be enemy, could be a religious man, and could be Muslim. You keep deceiving yourself. You hide under Bible.

And you keep saying Jesus, Jesus is love, whereas inside your pocket Jesus is your enemy. Love is greater than everything you practice. Are the Muslims the ones condemning me? Are they the ones speaking against me? Are they the ones saying you should not come here?

Why are we deceiving ourselves? Where there is love you come to me, and I will come to you. You want to know what I am doing and I want to know what you are doing. The Bible says, "Find out the truth and the truth shall set you free."

HE IS A GOD OF POSSIBILITIES

"Our God is a God of possibility"[4] are the words of the man who introduced T. B. Joshua at the crusade in Australia in 2006.

This echoes T. B. Joshua's words that I cited in chapter 1. "We cannot get beyond God's miracle," he said. "So, you should expect something beyond human understanding."

Loving God means a hunger to do his will, to listen to him, and to be open to his direction. In Mark 7:9, Jesus warns against setting aside the commands of God for the sake of our traditions. That was the issue facing Nicodemus when he came to Jesus in the remarkable encounter recorded in the Gospel of John. Prophet T. B. Joshua spoke about him in a short message at the Australian meeting. He began by reading from John 3.

> Now there was a man of the Pharisees named Nicodemus, a member of the Jewish ruling council. He came to Jesus by night and said, "Rabbi, we know that you are a teacher who has come from God, for no one could perform the miraculous signs you are doing if God were not with him."
>
> In reply Jesus declared, "I tell you the truth; no one can see the kingdom of God unless he is born again. How can a man be born when he is old?"
>
> Nicodemus asked, "Surely, he cannot enter a second time into his mother's womb to be born!"
>
> Jesus answered, "I tell you the truth; no one can enter the kingdom of God unless he is born of water and the Spirit. Flesh gives birth to flesh, but the Spirit gives birth to spirit. You should not be surprised at my saying, 'You must be born again.'" (John 3:1-7 [NIV])
>
> Going by what Nicodemus said to Jesus, he certainly had some prejudice. This means there was some arguments, disputes, somewhere

about Jesus Christ. I mean, a kind of mindset about Jesus. That is, the opinions of people were not the same. Some would say, "He is a good man."

Others would say, "No, he deceives people." People always fight what they do not understand. What they do not understand, they call names. What they understand, they destroy.

This was the situation that Nicodemus found himself in. Being a man of principle, he decided to make sure of all things before he could hold fast to that which is fine. He decided to find out the truth. He did not sit somewhere and hear this and that and then come to a hasty conclusion. He knew that knowing God is not only seeing His work but learning His way.

Today, many develop love because of what they hear about a particular person. Many develop hatred because of what they hear about a particular person they have never met. Nicodemus was never such a person. He was not the kind of man to be swayed by what people said. He was not the kind of person to be deceived by what he read.

When he met Jesus, he did not discuss state affairs as a ruler. Rather, he acknowledged his ignorance. He acknowledged his weakness which showed a genuine desire to learn and be better informed. To know God's strength, we must know our weakness. Jesus did not complain of his coming in the night. Jesus knew that if something must grow, it must start little.

If one's faith is to grow, it must start in a weak form. Remember, you were once a tiny embryo. See what you have become today. Glory be to God! Let us look at Christians who are weak in faith. "We who are strong ought to bear with the failings of the weak and not to please ourselves. Each of us should please his neighbor for his good, to build him up. For even Christ did not please himself, but as it is written: 'The insults of those who insult you have fallen on me.' " (Romans 15:1-3). "One man considers one day more sacred than another; another man considers every day alike. Each one should be fully convinced in his own mind."(Rom. 14:5 [NIV])

"For anything that does not come from faith is sin." (Rom. 14:23 [NIV])

What are the things that do not come from faith? Whatever you hear that is not examined in the light of God's Word does not come from faith. Whatever you see that is not examined in the light of God's Word does not come from faith. Whatever you read that is not examined in the light of God's Word does not come from faith.

Therefore, any moment from now whatever you are going to see in terms of miracles, don't ask your neighbor, "What is this?"

Everyone lies to his neighbor. Whatever you see, whatever you read, whatever you hear about this meeting, should be examined in the light of God's Word because everyone lies to his neighbor. We are in a danger zone. Let me take you to the Book of Psalms. Psalm 12:2, "Everyone lies to his neighbor. Their flattering lips speak with deception."

If everyone lies to his neighbor, it means unfaithful friends are around you. What does the Bible mean? It means everything you hear must be examined in the light of God's Word. This is the kind of situation we find ourselves in this world today. Always ask, What does God's Word say about this situation?

Among the distinguished panel that welcomed T. B. Joshua to the 2006 Australia crusade was the Honorable Alan Cadman, federal member of Parliament. Alan Cadman carried a message of welcome from the Prime Minister of Australia, Hon. John Howard. The Honorable Louise Marcus, federal minister of Parliament also welcomed Prophet T. B. Joshua.

The visit was also graced by Mayor of Blacktown, Sydney, Mr. Leonard Kelly.

The Rev. Peter Walker, chairman of the Aboriginal community in Sydney said he could see the fulfilment of the Book of Acts. "I just sense that awesome presence of God right now."

Who would have imagined such an occasion when T. B. Joshua first announced the birth of the Synagogue Church of All Nations in 1989?

"Everything big starts little," he said in Australia. That could be interpreted in two ways. It's the story of the humble beginnings of the ministry. It is also a story of the future that was yet to unfold. The size of the Australian meeting was quite modest. The international outreach of the ministry was just beginning.

LET US THEREFORE LIVE TOGETHER IN LOVE

One should not speak against persons based on hearsay, as T. B. Joshua reminded us through the story of Nicodemus. According to the dictionary definition, hearsay is information received from other people that one cannot adequately substantiate. Other associated terms or synonyms are rumor, gossip, tittle-tattle, idle chatter, idle talk, mere talk, tales, tidbits, and the grapevine.

> There is a problem. Insincerity. Let us live together in love. We are known by our love. God will never commit the grace to heal others when you do not love. Because if God gives that grace to you, you will not bless your enemy. God says love your neighbor as yourself. Your neighbor can be your enemies. God is the rewarder of love. When you love you are not expecting money, reverence, or adoration from the person you bless. (T. B. Joshua)

OUR UTMOST FOR THE HIGHEST.

T. B. Joshua's vision of a Church of All Nations has been a revelation of the unfolding grace of God as He prepares the world for the return of His Son, our Lord Jesus Christ. The story we have witnessed has the face of T. B. Joshua, but it is not about him. God has used him and others to point to something more, something greater, and something of great splendor. His message reminds us of who we are, what we ought to be, and what our future holds.

> What do you expect from God? The world is upside down. If you don't look at me by faith, you see Mr. T. B. Joshua. If you look at me in faith, you see Prophet T. B. Joshua. How many of you have faith eyes …? Without faith, how will you look at the man? How will you receive? I pray your faith will not fail. (T. B. Joshua)

And now, the challenge to re-examine ourselves.

> What are you doing that brings hope to people, joy to the sad, blessing to the poor, healing to the sick? What are you doing that changes lives, changes nations, and changes the world? Is it a crime to make people hear? Can your god do that? If your god cannot do that, your

god can make one deaf. It's either your god opens one's ears, or he can make one deaf. If your god cannot open, your god will close. There are two channels. Channel to open and channel to close. That is the question. The world will be at peace if I touch your weakness and give you strength, and you give me strength where I am weak. (T. B. Joshua)

Richard Wurmbrand (1909-2001) the founder of Voice of the Martyrs said, "We have experienced a new form of Christianity. The kind where Christ's love conquers all."[5]

This is the Spirit that carried the apostles and prophets of old. This is the Spirit that has carried T. B. Joshua. May this experience be mirrored in all our hearts.

CHAPTER 13

AFTERWORD: THE FUTURE TO BELIEVE IN

With the passing on of T. B. Joshua, the leadership of the Synagogue Church of All Nations transitioned to his wife and disciple, Mrs. Evelyn Joshua. Very little has been known of T. B. Joshua's family outside the ministry circles. A case in point is a BBC story that claimed that T. B. Joshua's sons "were known to be heading branches."

The reality is that there are three daughters, and no sons. I did query the report with a BBC Africa editor, and their response was, "We were told that T. B. Joshua had sons but following your email have not been able to confirm it, so we have amended the copy to children."[1]

Mrs. Evelyn Joshua announced her appointment as the leader of the Synagogue Church of All Nation in a statement broadcast on Emmanuel TV.[2] The following is a text of her statement.

> Emmanuel! God is with us. My name is Evelyn Joshua. I am pleased to address you at this moment upon my appointment as the leader of the Synagogue Church of All Nations.
>
> To all our members, partners, friends, and compatriots of faith, I say good morning and win today. It has been three months since the glorious home call of our dear father, founder and general overseer, Senior Prophet Temitope Balogun Joshua, which occurred on June 5, 2021.

These past three months have surely been challenging, but we thank you all for remaining strong and for keeping the faith as we have been trained, built, instructed, and taught by God's servant himself that trials are the soil upon which faith flourishes. We salute your faith.

Today, like always, is a new dawn in the Synagogue Church of All Nations. As we all know, Prophet T. B. Joshua fought his good fight of the kingdom and finished strong to the glory of God.

We have now commenced the journey from where our father left the baton. He had already prepared us all for this new phase and we must rise up to the occasion as a team under the command of God and the direction of the Holy Spirit. The journey is for us all. The Synagogue Church of All Nations cannot be without you, all the members, partners and friends of the ministry. So, this now serves as a clarion call for you all to rise as an army of God as we push this great commission forward.

I am not your general overseer. My dear husband and our dear father, the prophet for generations, Senior Prophet T. B. Joshua remains the founder and general overseer of the Synagogue Church of All Nations. Like my beloved husband used to say, "Let love lead."

Today, I represent the symbol of that love, even as he continues to reside by the right-hand side of his Maker.

17. Pastor Evelyn Joshua at the SCOAN

I am only a servant, who under the leadership and direction of the Holy Spirit, will team up with you all to direct the affairs of this great ministry. We will work together, pray together, fight the fight of faith together, win together so that we can all inherit the everlasting home together.

I know that we have all missed the congregation of our brethren for the past one and a half years, but let me assure you that as God leads, we shall all soon converge again and worship God together as a family.

So, watch out! There is no gain saying the fact that I and the entire team need your prayers, support, encouragement and advice at this time. The duty is much, the burden is heavy, but we will all cast them unto Jesus, who has already given a promise of His help.

I thank you all once again for the love and support you have shown to this Ministry and Senior Prophet T.B. Joshua for the past years. But if there is any time to show that love more, the time is now. Let me again assure you, as it has always been the watchword of this Ministry, that God is always with us. Emmanuel! God bless you all. Thank you.

MRS. EVELYN JOSHUA, WIFE AND DISCIPLE

The most complete profile of Evelyn Joshua was a result of a 2009 interview she gave to Nigerian journalists Chika Abanobi and Shola Oshunkeye. A transcript of the interview is published by the Synagogue Church of All Nations.[3] In the interview, she spoke warmly of her husband and the qualities that bonded them from the earliest days.

"He is a God-fearing man," she said. "I saw a kind-hearted man, a zealous man, a man of one purpose, a man with a sole aim to please God at all times, with every other thing being secondary. I think those qualities were what cemented our relationship."

The wedding took place in 1990.

Mrs. Evelyn Joshua is also known through a select number of messages she has given during the Sunday service. One such sermon is entitled "The Future to Believe In." In this, and other messages, she naturally rhymes with her husband in thought and expression.

T. B. Joshua trained many other disciples, many of whom are not currently known to the wider world. They shall be known by their fruit.

NOTES

AUTHOR'S PROLOGUE

1. *TB Joshua mission accomplished.* YouTube video, 2:30. Posted by Testimony of Jesus." December 20, 2021. https://www.youtube.com/watch?v=b86uoctu2vo

CHAPTER 1

1. "Untold Story of a Mystery Prophet T. B. Joshua." The Sun. Reproduced on the SCOAN blog, June 3, 2009, https://www.scoan.org/blog/2009/06/03/untold-story-of-a-mystery-prophet-tb-joshua-the-sun/

2. T. B. Joshua, "My stopping interval," SCOAN International (blog) October 5, 2009, https://www.scoan.org/blog/2009/10/05/my-stopping-interval/

3. T. B. Joshua 2009, "My stopping interval."

4. *This Is My Story: T. B. Joshua's Documentary.* 1:10:09. Posted by "Rejoice and See," February 2, 2022. https://youtu.be/15qIRI_jG2Q

5. *Documentary about the building of the SCOAN Cathedral.* YouTube video, 30.26. Posted by "Rejoice and See," January 31, 2022. https://www.youtube.com/watch?v=LLv7W_iYtWE&t=10s

6. The team was made up of Pastor Arie Potuyt and Bert Panhuise, chairman of EuroSpirit, both from Rotterdam,Netherlands. It is my understanding that the recording was not aired as originally planned as a result of controversies that arose in the Netherlands. I discuss this in chapter 9. But the interview itself is very straightforward and clear. The video is posted on YouTube. See *T. B. Joshua's interview twenty years ago.* You video, 17:29, posted by "Rejoice and See," February 2, 2022, https://youtu.be/4HP_OXh4lQM

CHAPTER 2

1. *Christianity is a relationship.* YouTube video, 34.08. Posted by "Rejoice and See," January 31, 2022. https://www.youtube.com/watch?v=YBgS2jTiyx4&t=261s

2. *The Secret Behind Miracles.* YouTube video ,40:22. Posted by "Rejoice and See," January 31, 2022, https://youtu.be/-AbhXKymFME

3. *Believe and be filled with the Holy Spirit,* YouTube video, 31.04. Posted by "Rejoice and See," January 31, 2022 https://youtu.be/IEozcU1YR5g

4. I have used the Prophet's words. I have also made some minor edits as needed to adapt the text to an audience readers.

5. *The Secret Behind Miracles.*

6. *Pastors Conference With Prophet T. B. Joshua In Colombia*. YouTube video, 46.24. Posted by "Rejoice and See," February 2, 2022 https://youtu.be/fQBG4kU3aHo

7. *Prophet T. B. Joshua rebukes the church in stinging sermon*, YouTube video, 23.07. Posted by "Rejoice and See" February 2, 2022. https://youtu.be/_EH7e85kse4

8. *Believe and be filled with the Holy Spirit*

9. *Prophet T. B. Joshua rebukes the church in stinging sermon*, YouTube video, 23.07. Posted by "Rejoice and See" February 2, 2022. https://youtu.be/_EH7e85kse4

10. *Prophet T. B. Joshua rebukes the church in stinging sermon.*

11. *New Year Message From Prophet T. B. Joshua 2016*. YouTube video, 39.45. Posted by "Rejoice and See" February 2, 2022 https://youtu.be/Qqq2cTZVOFk

12. *How to forgive someone who has hurt you deeply*. YouTube video, 17:15. Posted by "Rejoice and See" January 31, 2022 https://www.youtube.com/watch?v=q8gYdDOIT3k

CHAPTER 3

1. Woman reveals TB Joshua's secret formula for success. YouTube video,18:40. Posted by "Rejoice and See" January 29, 2022 https://youtu.be/Yz1OdP431nQ

2. *The Benefit of Failure*. YouTube video, 32.24. Posted by "Rejoice and See" February 2, 2022 https://youtu.be/Co2klQF1SpM

3. *T. B. Joshua: Forgive This Man: The Power of Forgiveness*. YouTube video, 20:18. Posted by "Rejoice and See" February 3, 2022 https://youtu.be/bqqv5OHgqQ0

4. *T. B. Joshua: Forgive This Man: The Power of Forgiveness.*

5. *This Marriage Reconciliation Will Melt Your Heart*. YouTube video, 23:39. Posted by "Rejoice and See" February 3, 2022, https://youtu.be/W1HUDfJXD5o

6. It takes a while to get used to how T. B. Joshua moves and sees. He clearly sees more than the people around him

CHAPTER 4

1. *Evangelist Bill Subritzky's Testimony About T.B. Joshua*, YouTube video, 8:44. Posted by "Rejoice and See" February 3, 2022 https://youtu.be/xiQAqxoDZIw

2. *C. S. Upthegrove. God's General C. S. Upthegrove Visits Prophet T. B. Joshua*. YouTube video, 36:50. Posted by "Rejoice and See" March 2, 2022 https://youtu.be/tbZds3V82gw

CHAPTER 5

1. *Watch T. B. Joshua Sermon: Who is a Prophet*. YouTube video, 8:40. Posted by "Rejoice and See," Feb 13, 2022. https://youtu.be/Iphbr4220Ug

2. *Shameful secrets exposed*. YouTube video, Feb 13, 2022. Posted by "Rejoice and See," Feb 13, 2022, https://youtu.be/ngdKvw_Ev4E

3. *Shameful secrets exposed.*

4. *Your Girlfriend Is In Church While Your Wife Is At Home*. YouTube video, 6:39. Posted by "Rejoice and See," Feb 13, 2022, https://youtu.be/-KGI4RSQKgo

5. *Prostitute restored*. YouTube video, 18:41. Posted by "Rejoice and See," Feb 13, 2022. https://youtu.be/u0hmxfuyn2s

CHAPTER 6

1. SCOAN. Prophecy for 2020 –Prophet T. B. Joshua. January 5, 2020. https://www.scoan.org/blog/2020/01/05/prophecy-for-2020-prophet-tb-joshua/

2. Aubri Juhasz. Queen Elizabeth II Calls A Family Meeting To Determine Meghan and Harry's Next Steps. January 12, 2020. NPR News. https://www.npr.org/2020/01/12/795690915/queen-elizabeth-ii-calls-a-family-meeting-to-determine-meghan-and-harrys-next-st

3. BBC News. Meghan and Harry interview: Urgent Palace talks over claims, March 9, 2020. https://www.bbc.com/news/uk-56329887

4. SCOAN. Prophecy for 2020 –Prophet T. B. Joshua. January 5, 2020. https://www.scoan.org/blog/2020/01/05/prophecy-for-2020-prophet-tb-joshua/

5. *Don't figh Syria*, YouTube video, 13:03. Posted by "Rejoice and See," Feb 13, 2022. https://youtu.be/Hp70e6Tbbds

6. *Prophecy on terrorism Worldwide.* YouTube video, 14:22. Posted by "Rejoice and See," Jan 29, 2022 https://youtu.be/4a2pIfInmQI

7. Bethan McKernan. "Up to 30,000 ISIS Fighters Remain in Iraq and Syria, Says UN," *Independent,* 15 August, 2018, https://www.independent.co.uk/news/world/middle-east/isis-fighters-iraq-syria-un-report-jihadis-raqqa-iraq-a8492736.html

8. Elizabeth McLaughlin, Conor Finnegan, and Bader Katy. "US Military Resumes Operations Against ISIS in Iraq After Pause Due to Iran Tensions," *ABC News,* January 16, 2020. https://abcnews.go.com/Politics/us-military-resumes-operations-isis-iraq-pause-due/story?id=68327403

9. *Prophet T. B. Joshua At The Altar.* YouTube video, 1:28:00. Posted by "Rejoice and See," Jan 29, 2022 https://youtu.be/XJHJSVuzhJc

10. PRI. "Nigerian President Goodluck Jonathan Loses, Makes History." Transcript. https://www.pri.org/node/78928/popout

11. *Prophet T. B. Joshua At The Altar.*

CHAPTER 7

1. *Testimony of restoration.* YouTube video, 31.59. Posted by "Rejoice and See," March 2, 2022. https://youtu.be/FJLVO_QBoKQ

2. See Willem J. Ouweneel, "Wonderen en tekenen." Transl. Jan H. Boer. Sophie, September 2013, pp. 32-35, http://www.socialtheology.com/docs/ouweneel-wonders-090013.pdf

3. *Miracle is for the salvation of your soul.* YouTube video, 1:59:53. Posted by "Rejoice and See," Feb 13, 2022 https://youtu.be/maYwDU_Yp1Y

4. *Medical Doctor Injured at the Gym Walks* Again. YouTube video, 18:30. Posted by "Rejoice and See," Feb 13, 2022 https://youtu.be/kzOiHCg2SBA

5. *Watch an Astounding Healing of Deafness.* YouTube video, 8:08. Posted by "Rejoice and See," Feb 13, 2022 https://youtu.be/fUT58SSezpk

6. *Medical Doctor Healed of Writer's Spasm & Delivered From Nightmares.* YouTube video, 15:26. Posted by "Rejoice and See," Feb 14, 2022 https://youtu.be/EaL_qTpeYxA

7. *Prophecy Time & Deliverance with T. B. Joshua.* YouTube video, 1:58:58. Posted by "Rejoice and See," Feb 14, 2022, https://youtu.be/ja9TPfhz5OI

8. *The Life Changing Testimony of a Boy Whose Family Were Slaughtered By Armed Robbers.* YouTube video, 2:15:06. Posted by "Rejoice and See," February 14, 2022. https://youtu.be/075yUVmQEuY

9. *Strange Skin Disease Deliverance* YouTube video, 13:2. Posted by "Rejoice and See," Feb 14, 2022, https://youtu.be/_5MGpGPb7JQ

10. This undercuts the argument that the SCOAN presents a false alternative. People tend to come there as a last resort. They have more faith in hospitals, and in native doctors. In local colloquialism, they mostly talk of the SCOAN as the 'Last Bus Stop"; that is the place of last resort when everything has failed. There are therefore important questions about how the level of faith that the typical person coming to the SCOAN has as they enter the church for the first time. Is it therefore surprising when T. B. Joshua throws up his arms and says, "I don't see Christians here?"

11. Observers of the SCOAN will notice that vomiting/throwing up is one of the core mechanisms through which healing occurs.

12. *Man Healed Of Colon Cancer & Delivered From Smoking Addiction*. YouTube video, 34:57. Posted by "Momisi," Feb 14, 2022. https://youtu.be/U-FpekVZGq4

13. *Testimony of Mrs Rauna Kakehongo healed of blood and bone marrow cancer*. YouTube video, 56:40. Posted by "Rejoice and See," Feb 14, 2022, https://youtu.be/VRgR8OfvIXI

14. *Healed of Ovarian Cancer Jesus' Name*. YouTube video, 9:28. Posted by "Rejoice and See," Feb 14, 2022. https://youtu.be/nY_HwNQvwqY

15. T. B. Joshua has maintained a comprehensive archive.

16. Rowan Moore Gerety, "Only the Synagogue Can Save You." *Foreign Policy.* April 25, 2014. https://foreignpolicy.com/2014/04/25/only-the-synagogue-can-save-you/

17. *Horrific: A Bloody Miracle*. YouTube video, 27:31. Posted by "Rejoice and See," Feb 14, 2022, https://youtu.be/6cYmr5A00EA

18. See *Horrific: A Bloody Miracle*. The blood gush start at 2:20 minutes.

19. *T. B. Joshua Revelation Words*. YouTube video, 2:26:02. Posted by "Rejoice and See," Feb 14, 2022. https://youtu.be/E7H8JYy86H4

CHAPTER 8

1. Ukah, Asonzeh., "Banishing miracles: Politics and policies of religious broadcasting in Nigeria." *Politics and Religion Journal* 5.1 (2011): 39-60. See also Helen Baker, "Emmanuel TV: Celebrating a decade of blessings." March 8, 2016 *PM News*. https://www.pmnewsnigeria.com/2016/03/08/emmanuel-tv-celebrating -a-decade-of-blessings-by-helen-baker/

2. *T. B. Joshua Gives Homeless Man a Beautiful Surprise*. YouTube video, 21:19. YouTube video, 21:19. Posted by "Rejoice and See," March 2, 2022 https://youtu.be/3kI0ALG09A0

3. See for example, Anna Momigliano, *About 150 Migrants Drown in Shipwreck Off Libya*. New York Times, July 25, 2019. https://www.nytimes.com/2019/07/25/world/middleeast/migrants-shipwreck-libya.html

4. *Sunday Live Service "Prophet T. B. Joshua Speaks"* YouTube video, 53:03. Posted by "Rejoice and See," Feb 14, 2022. https://youtu.be/01GPMKRGTsg

5. *"I lost My Kidney Sleeping With Men" Prostitute Confession*. YouTube video, 9:30. Posted by "Rejoice and See," Feb 5, 2022. https://youtu.be/K2oxFsh400A

6. Doctors Removed Kidney, God Blesses With A New One. YouTube video, 14:00. Posted by "Rejoice and See," Feb 16, 2022. https://youtu.be/E_6ZgXSBi18

7. T. B. Joshua Ministries. "T. B. Joshua receives ambassador of peace award," April 4, 2013, Facebook. https://www.facebook.com/tbjministries/photos/ tb-joshua-receives-ambassador-of-peace-awardthe-arewa-youth-form-northern-nigeri/440502276070554/

8. See SCOAN, *Roadmap: Reaching out to a troubled world*. Lagos: SCOAN

9. "SCOAN – A Refuge For All Nations. " (Blog) February 24, 2013, https://www.scoan.org/blog/2013/02/26/a-new-life/

CHAPTER 9

1. T B Joshua "A cloud that covers Nigeria as close as my mouth." Bomb. YouTube video, 2:45. Posted by "Rejoice and See," Feb 16, 2022 https://youtu.be/r3BFFumQUX0

2. *Shocking Confession of Boko Haram Member Emmanuel.* YouTube video, 19:03 Posted by "Rejoice and See," Feb 16, 2022, https://youtu.be/jPnJMSux-5I

3. *Boko Haram Member Delivered & Excreted Poisonous Substances.* YouTube video, 29:38. Posted by "Rejoice and See," Published on Feb 16,2022. https://youtu.be/pdvKUHMkfXY

4. *SCOAN Building Collapse – Security cameras.* YouTube video, 12:21. Posted by "Rejoice and See," Feb 16,2022 https://youtu.be/XsyxH8TW1-s

5. T. B. Joshua releases another video of Synagogue building collapse, YouTube video, 8:34. Posted by "Rejoice and See," Jan 31,2022 https://youtu.be/Csh7QvS9x8k

6. One is eerily reminded of T. B. Joshua's statement after his return from Colombia: "But if anything bad happens in front of the church, one of you Nigerians will be the one to make a call. You are destroying your country, selling your country at nothing. It's a very painful thing."

7. Nkrumah Bankong-Obi. "U.S. Varsity Dons Want T.B. Joshua Tried." *PM News.* September 25, 2014 https://www.pmnewsnigeria.com/2014/09/25/u-s-varsity-dons-want-t-b-joshua-tried/

8. Foundation of collapsed Synagogue building not defective, witness tells court." March 22, 2019. https://pmnewsnigeria.com/2019/03/22/ foundation-of-collapsed-synagogue-building-not-defective-witness-tells-court/

CHAPTER 10

1. See for example, Jaja, J. (2016). "Stomach Infrastructure in His Name: A Critique of Pentecostalism." *Elixir Social Studies, 95,* 41192-41204.

2. See for example *T. B. Joshua, How pastors pay tithes,* YouTube video, 2:39. Posted by "Rejoice and See," Feb 16, 2022. https://youtu.be/O3l0ci8cEQQ or Olayinka. "T.B Joshua has finally spoken truth on tithe," December 3, 2017 https://www.informationng.com/2017/12/t-b-joshua-finally-spoken-truth-tithe-oap-freeze-video.html

3. The Eagle Online, "T.B. Joshua shocks mammoth crowd at UK crusade: Give your offering to your neighbour", June 7, 2019. https://theeagleonline.com.ng/t-b-joshua-shocks-mammoth-crowd-at-uk -crusade-give-your-offering-to-your-neighbour/

4. *The. Warning God Gave TB Joshua.* YouTube video, 18:34. Posted by "Rejoice and See," February 16,2022. https://youtu.be/Woj-pU8N4lk

5. *The danger in collecting offering.* YouTube video, 14:36. Posted by "Rejoice and See," Jan 20, 2022. https://youtu.be/rmqVkkyaRuE

6. Andy Dangerfield, Church HIV prayer cure claim 'cause three deaths.' *BBC News.,* 18 October 2011. https://www.bbc.com/news/uk-england-london-14406818

7. Wikipedia. "T. B. Joshua." https://en.wikipedia.org/wiki/T._B._Joshua. See also Infogalctic Planetary Knowledge Core. "T. B. Joshua" https://infogalactic.com/info/T._B._Joshua

8. Ray Downs. "Church Claiming It Can 'Pray the AIDS Away' Blamed for 6 Premature Deaths." *Christian Post.* November 28, 2011, https://www.christianpost.com/news/church-claiming-it-can-pray-the-aids-away-blamed-for-6-premature-deaths-video.html

9. Sahara Reporters, "Millionaire Nigerian Pastor T. B. Joshua's Church Linked To Fraudulent AIDS Claims." October, 19, 2011, http://saharareporters.com/2011/10/19/millionaire-nigerian-pastor-tb-joshuas-church-linked-fraudulent-aids-claims

10. Speakman, Sloane. "Comparing the Impact of Religious Discourse on HIV/AIDS in Islam and Christianity in Africa." *Vanderbilt Undergraduate Research Journal* 8 (2012).

11. Rowan Moore Gerety. "Only the Synagogue Can Save You." *Foreign Policy.* April 25, 2014.
    https://foreignpolicy.com/2014/04/25/only-the-synagogue-can-save-you/

12. The IRP folded in 2018, citing lack of funding support.

13. Gerard ter Horst. "T. B. Joshua to the Netherlands?" 13 May 2005.
    https://vergadering.nu/leesmap20050513-tbjoshua.htm

14. Jerrell Miller, *Remnant International* http://www.theremnant.com/news.html

15. J. Lee Grady. "Nigerian Healer T.B. Joshua Still Attracts Followers From Abroad." *Charisma* magazine.
    2004.
    https://www.charismamag.com/site-archives/154-peopleevents/
    people-and-events/1086-nigerian-healer-tb-joshua-still-attracts-followers-from-abroad

16. See for example, Ruth Marshall, "Political spiritualities : the Pentecostal revolution in Nigeria. 2009."
    University of Chicago Press; J. Lee Grady. 2002. "Church Leaders Still at Odds Over Credibility of Faith
    Healer T.B. Joshua," Charisma. https://www.charismamag.com/site-archives/154-peopleevents/people-and-
    events/758-church-leaders-still-at-odds-over-credibility-of-faith-healer-tb-joshua. The meeting also features
    on the Wikipedia profile of T. B. Joshua.

17. J. Lee Grady, "Famed Nigerian Faith Healer 'Dangerous to the Body of Christ'", 2002.
    http://www.toetsalles.nl/htmldoc/bio.joshua.charisma2.htm

18. J. Lee Grady, "Famed Nigerian Faith Healer 'Dangerous to the Body of Christ'"

19. J. Lee Grady. 2002. "Church Leaders Still at Odds Over Credibility of Faith Healer
    T.B. Joshua," *Charisma,* https://www.charismamag.com/site-archives/154-peopleevents/
    people-and-events/758-church-leaders-still-at-odds-over-credibility-of-faith-healer-tb-joshua.

20. J. Lee Grady, Famed Nigerian Faith Healer 'Dangerous to the Body of Christ' 2002.
    http://www.toetsalles.nl/htmldoc/bio.joshua.charisma2.htm

21. J. Lee Grady, Famed Nigerian Faith Healer 'Dangerous to the Body of Christ' 2002.

22. Sam Eyoboka and John Ighodaro, "Nigeria: Okotie, Oyakhilome Rift: Pfn Disowns T.B. Joshua," 15
    November 2001 https://allafrica.com/stories/200111150478.html

23. Sam Eyoboka and John Ighodaro, "Nigeria: Okotie, Oyakhilome Rift: Pfn Disowns T.B. Joshua."

24. Magbadelo, J.O. (2004) Pentecostalism in Nigeria: Exploiting or edifying the masses? African sociological
    review 8(2) 15-29

25. Ukah, Asonzeh. "Banishing miracles: Politics and policies of religious broadcasting in Nigeria." *Politics and
    Religion Journal* 5, no. 1 (2011): 39-60.

26. Magbadelo, J.O. (2004) "Pentecostalism in Nigeria: Exploiting or edifying the masses?" *African sociological
    review* 8(2) 15-29

27. Ukah, Asonzeh. "Banishing miracles: Politics and policies of religious broadcasting in Nigeria. Although
    Uka also mentions Chris Oyakhilome of Believers' Loveworld, the record shows that T. B. Joshua was the
    target. See Sam Eyoboka and John Ighodaro, "Nigeria: Okotie, Oyakhilome Rift: Pfn Disowns T.B. Joshua."

28. J. Lee Grady, "Famed Nigerian Faith Healer 'Dangerous to the Body of Christ'"
    http://www.toetsalles.nl/htmldoc/bio.joshua.charisma2.htm

29. *J. Lee Grady.* Famed Nigerian Faith Healer 'Dangerous to the Body of Christ'.

30. J. Lee Grady, "The Lost Gift of Discernment," Frontier Harvest Ministrires Blog, September 5, 2008,
    https://frontierharvestministries.blogspot.com/2008/09/j-lee-grady-lost-gift-of-discernment.html

31. J. Lee Grady, "Nigerian Healer T.B. Joshua Still Attracts Followers From Abroad."
    Charisma. Nov 30, 2003. http://www.charismamag.com/site-archives/154-peopleevents/
    people-and-events/1086-nigerian-healer-tb-joshua-still-attracts-followers-from-abroad

32. J. Lee Grady. "The Lost Gift of Discernment."

33. Hanke Helms, "T. B. Joshua-Healings in Nigeria." *Nederlands Dagblad,* 20-4-2002. https://vergadering.nu/leesmap20020420wjoinlagosnd.htm

34. *Jan Westerhof healed of MS, 2002.* YouTube video, 26:11. Posted by "Rejoice and See," March 2, 2022, https://youtu.be/prC6GpoDnNw (The Jan Westerhof miracle is about 16 minutes into the video).

35. see Tjerk W. Muller, "How I the T. B. Joshua phenomenon assessed?" The Hague, 2002. https://translate.google.com/translate?hl=en&sl=nl&u=http://www.apologetique.org/nl/artikelen/religie/heterodoxie/neomontanisme/TWM_tb_joshua.htm&prev=search

36. see Tjerk W. Muller, The Hague, 2002

37. see Tjerk W. Muller, The Hague, 2002

38. *T. B. Joshua's interview 20 years ago.* YouTube video, 17:30. Posted by "Rejoice and See," Feb 2, 2022, https://youtu.be/4HP_OXh4lQM

39. Tjerk W. Muller, "How I the T. B. Joshua phenomenon assessed?" The Hague, 2002. https://translate.google.com/translate?hl=en&sl=nl&u=http://www.apologetique.org/nl/artikelen/religie/heterodoxie/neomontanisme/TWM_tb_joshua.htm&prev=search.

40. See for example, Ayo Onikoyi. How other men of God see T. B. Joshua. Vanguard. September 27, 2024. https://www.vanguardngr.com/2014/09/men-god-see-tb-joshua/

41. A photograph attributed to a Sandy Simpson is a surprise inclusion in the article by Tjerk W. Muller. The picture has the face of T. B. Joshua, standing by an image with the words, "There is no deity (God) but Allah." The word, "Quran" can be made out but faintly. Anyone who is properly acquainted with T. B. Joshua can tell the image is a fake. The image has been used to spread fiction about T. B. Joshua's faith and his ministry. The inclusion of the picture by Muller is a surprise because he is ostensibly writing to a thoughtful audience and he has some standing in the scholarly community. His predisposition to judge T. B. Joshua seems to have clouded his judgment of sources. One can tell that he sourced the picture from an online piece by Simpson entitled "T. B. Joshua: To Deceive Even The Elect." In that article, it is clear that Simpson was not personally acquainted with T. B. Joshua or the SCOAN. He claimed to have obtained the picture from an unnamed source in South Africa.

42. Tjerk W. Muller, "How Is the T. B. Joshua phenomenon assessed?" The Hague, 2002. [translation of Dutch. Hoe beoordeelt men het verschijnsel T.B. Joshua?] http://www.apologetique.org/nl/artikelen/religie/heterodoxie/neomontanisme/TWM_tb_joshua.htm

CHAPTER 11

1. This chapter is based on the messages, (1) *Discover the secret of bringing Jesus in the scene.* YouTube video, 42.17. Posted by "Rejoice and See," Feb 16, 2022. https://youtu.be/2-RZpK2tUdc *(2) How to counsel yourself.* YouTube video, 48.15. Posted by "Rejoice and See," Feb 17, 2022. https://youtu.be/bmCzb4xnzDE

2. In his reference to Paul, Prophet T. B. Joshua had in mind 2 Corinthians 1, especially verses 8-11. "We do not want you to be uninformed, brothers and sisters about the troubles we in the province of Asia. We were under great experienced pressure, far beyond our ability to endure so that we despaired of life itself," Paul writes.

3. *How to counsel yourself.* YouTube video.

CHAPTER 12

1. T. B. Joshua. "Love without expectation." *SCOAN international* (blog), Jan 14, 2016, https://www.scoan.org/blog/2016/01/14/love-without-expectation/

2. *How I respond to critics.* YouTube video, 2:07. Posted by "Rejoice and See," February 17, 2022. https://youtu.be/lwWgimEfils

3. *Shocking confession of a Nigerian Pastor*. YouTube video, 43.13. Posted by "Rejoice and See," Feb 17, 2022. https://youtu.be/2qB13UBxU0A

4. *T.B. Joshua in Australia - "Everything Big Starts Little."* YouTube video, 14:13. Posted by "Rejoice and See," Feb 17, 2022. https://youtu.be/lhZ3hEonQ9c

5. *Tortured for Christ,* Directed by John Grooters. Grooters Production, 2018. View online at https://www.persecution.com/tfcmovieevent/

CHAPTER 13

1. See Nduka Orjinmo. "T. B. Joshua: The Nigerian outsider who became a global televangelist star." https://www.bbc.com/news/world-africa-57388592

2. *A special address by Mrs. Evelyn Joshua,* YouTube video, 4:45. Posted by "Rejoice and See," Feb 17, 2022. https://youtu.be/LG_h2_XXDoY

3. The mystery woman who charmed T. B. Joshua, https://www.scoan.org/blog/2009/06/07/the-mystery-woman-who-charmed-tb-joshua/ June 7, 2009.

To learn more about Prophet T. B. Joshua Ministries:

Facebook.com/tbjministries

Watch Emmanuel Television on:

www.emmanuel.tv

For more on this book visit

www.rejoice-and-see.com

www.ingramcontent.com/pod-product-compliance
Lightning Source LLC
Chambersburg PA
CBHW021211130726
47988CB00002B/610